Covensense

About the author

As one of the world's most famous witches, Patricia Crowther has devoted almost half a century to promoting the craft of the wise through her books, articles, lectures and regular appearances on television and radio. Initiated in 1960 by her close friend and confidante Gerald Gardner, Patricia continued his work in order to bring the age-old religion of the Goddess to its rightful place in the new age.

Today, she enjoys giving tarot consultations, advising would-be witches, spending time with craft friends and caring for her cat, Sheba.

By the same author:

The Witches Speak
The Secrets of Ancient Witchcraft
Witch Blood!
Witchcraft in Yorkshire
Lid Off the Cauldron
Witches Were For Hanging
The Zodiac Experience
From Stagecraft to Witchcraft
One Witch's World (Published in the USA as
High Priestess)

Covensense

Patricia Crowther

ROBERT HALE

First published in 2009 by Robert Hale, an imprint of
The Crowood Press Ltd, Ramsbury, Marlborough
Wiltshire SN8 2HR

www.crowood.com

Paperback edition 2018

© Patricia Crowther 2019

British Library Cataloguing-in-Publication Data
A catalogue record for this book is available from the British Library.

ISBN 978 0 7198 2869 0

Typeset in 10/13¼pt Palatino
by Derek Doyle & Associates, Shaw Heath
Printed and bound in India by Replika Press Pvt Ltd

Dark Teacher!
Tell me yet again, what hidden love doth lie
Beneath the exoteric type of thy philosophy?
'The Useful is the Beautiful.'

Leitch Ritchie

THE CHANGING

The path goes by the Naked Man
to forest traces ponies ran.
You hear the singing in the trees.
Is it singing? Is it bees?
Or the sound of restless seas
with plumes so white they crash
in flight of effervescent filigrees?

The boundaries blue within the line.
What is, is not, is ill defined.
The spaces blend twixst air and tree;
New Forest turns to Wilde Fairie

Edwyn

Contents

Acknowledgements

My very special thanks to Al Bassetti for his enthusiasm and encouragement during the preparation of this book; and to my partner Ian Lilleyman for providing artwork and the still centre of my world.

Thanks are also extended to Richard Middlebrook for allowing me to feature his enigmatic poem on the tarot.

Larry Jones deserves my grateful thanks for visiting Tunis and making arrangements for a gravestone and a memorial to be erected upon Gerald Gardner's grave.

Special mention must also be given to Philip Heselton for providing a photograph of Mrs Woodford-Grimes, and to Michael Doherty for his pictures of stone carvings in Sheffield.

I am also indebted to Andrea Peckett for finding the time in her busy life to type the manuscript together with my list of instructions; and to literary agents A.P. Watt for their prompt and positive information concerning poetry by Rudyard Kipling and G.K. Chesterton.

The jacket illustration artwork and composition was by John Harper after an earlier photograph of the author taken by Gerald Gardner in his covenstead in the Isle of Man.

Thanks are also due to the *News of the World* newspaper for permission to quote from articles published in February 1969.

The author has tried without success to find the copyright holder of a verse featured in *Immortal Britain*, a book by Alan V. Insole. She would be pleased to hear from him or her so that this omission can be rectified.

List of Illustrations

1. A gathering of occultists at the Savoy Hotel, London
2. Edith Woodford-Grimes
3. 'Scrying is a very worthwhile exercise to perform in the Circle'
4. Ian Lilleyman, at Donna Gardner's grave on the Isle of Man
5. Stone carving of the 'Green Man' on a building in Sheffield
6. Flower vase for use in Aphrodite's temple at Paphos
7. Stone carving on a building in Sheffield, thought to be 'Flora' – the Goddess of Spring
8. Chalk goddess from Grime's Graves Neolithic Flint Mines in Norfolk.
9. An unfinished painting by Gerald Gardner
10. The unmarked grave of Gerald Gardner
11. After the placement of a gravestone
12. 'The Magician', a painting by Gerald Gardner
13. Arnold Crowther's original cartoons of Gerald Gardner depicting how various people saw him. As seen by William Worrall, manager of the café at the Witchcraft Museum on the Isle of Man
14. As seen by the people of Castletown, Isle of Man.
15. As seen by the folklorist, Christina Hole
16. And by the Christian church!

Preface

During the last half-century, witches, pagans and those of other magical persuasions, including members of the various societies, clubs and universities to whom I have lectured, asked many different questions about witchcraft, magic, and the occult in general.

When Al Bassetti, a witch friend, rang me from the States, he asked if I would be agreeable to answering some of his queries concerning the Craft and allied subjects. I acquiesced and said I would do my best! He explained that although he held the position of High Priest and had been initiated by a genuine High Priestess down the line, there were still many aspects of the 'Craft of the Wise' that he did not know, or was unsure about, and that many witches in the USA were in similar positions.

I had met Al and his lovely wife, Cathy, and knew that his knowledge of the subject was considerable, but when a system of magic, which was once a secret tradition, is handed down through the years, some small details can be missed out, or forgotten. And, considering the speed with which the Old Religion has spread to different parts of the world over the last fifty years, this is understandable, but regrettable.

Al's questions were very searching ones and revealed the depth of his allegiance to the Craft. They also revealed that intelligent people cannot be fobbed off with glib, fabricated answers made up on the spur of the moment. I have found that if you do not know the answer to a question, it is best to say, 'I don't know'.

After all, a person can be very knowledgeable on a subject, yet fail to take on board some of its more subtle aspects, and this is especially so with regard to the Mysteries.

During our conversations, Al said that a 'question and answer' book would be an excellent idea. It took time for me to assimilate this suggestion, then I remembered a dear friend and bona fide High Priestess, Eileen Smith, who had also asked me lots of questions about the Craft in Britain. I recalled, too, the many letters I have received from different parts of the world, all asking questions of one kind or another which, providing they did not encroach upon oath-bound material and contained an SAE, were duly answered. I also remembered the questions posed by my own initiates over the years, in the same way that I had often put questions to Gerald Gardner and Jean MacDonald.

So, *Covensense* was duly written in the hope that it might be helpful to witches, pagans and other occultists. In it, I have answered, to the best of my ability, some of the many questions concerning the numerous facets and mysterious byways which surround the practices and beliefs of witchcraft, both ancient and modern.

1 The Magic Circle

Rudyard Kipling wrote:

> I keep six honest serving men
> (They taught me all I knew);
> Their names are What and Why and When
> And How and Where and Who . . .

These lines fit exactly the theme of this book, and witchcraft is certainly a subject which evokes more questions than most.

We begin with the Magic Circle – the fundamental basis of worship, ritual and magical practices for thousands of years. How this particular concept came into being, and why, is therefore the initial question to be discussed.

Patricia, can you tell us about how the Magic Circle came into being?

It would seem that the circle as a pattern for building was one of the easiest shapes in which to construct anything. Early humans would also notice that the sun and the full moon looked circular in shape, and that nothing in the heavens was square-shaped. Everything seemed to be made from circles or curves. The very earliest homesteads, after humans left the caves (mostly womb-shaped), were circular huts, as were their temples, or stone circles. And so the Magic Circle is as old as time itself and has been used throughout millennia for many different and diverse reasons. As a symbol, the circle is the most sacred concept known to humanity. When we look up at the stars, we see that the universe is constructed from orbs of light – from millions of suns and planets of a circular structure. So it would seem to be the perfect shape in the mind of the Godhead: the creator/creatrix of the universe.

The circle has no beginning and no ending; it can be used as a protection, a barrier against hostile vibrations, or a means of constraining or conserving magical forces. Ancient peoples observed the changing of the seasons, and also their recurrence. They saw constellations of stars appear and disappear, only to reappear again after a lapse of time. All this, combined with the seasons of growth and decay in nature, gave early humans a feeling of confidence as to future conditions, and thus knowledge of the nature year, and of time, was established.

The stone circle, a feature set in the wilds of the countryside, was born from the observations of our ancestors, and was a sacred place where meetings for many different reasons occurred. These included business matters, the celebration of family occasions such as a birth, the binding of a loving couple, and even a death, when the soul of the departed was winged upon its way with love.

It is thought that each of the stones in many stone circles was raised in the name of a particular individual: those people who were known for their talents or their leadership, either living or dead. Thus a circle would embody the vibrations and memories of a collection of souls and become a true representation of the people and/or families who had built it.

The positioning of stone circles, monoliths and stone avenues would seem to have been of the utmost importance. Much has been written about ley lines, underground streams and lines of energy which can be likened to the nerves and blood vessels within the body of Mother Earth. It has been suggested that these stone constructions were raised on parts of the Earth where ley lines crossed or intersected each other, *ergo*, where the power or energy was the strongest. Scientific work such as the Dragon Project in the late 1970s discovered energy anomalies, magnetic fields and startling light sources at many of the sites. The Rollright Stones in particular proved to be a rich revenue of such discoveries. It was found that the magnetic field within the stone circle was lower than that outside, and that this fluctuated over a period of hours. Ultrasonic pulsing was recorded at the circle's King stone at dawn in the autumn of 1978, and this was repeated in the circle at various times of the year, usually at dawn. An infra-red photograph taken of the King stone at sunrise in April of the following year disclosed a glow emanating from the stone, and a ray of light shooting off from it, which experts have yet to explain. This last phenomenon reminds me of the photograph taken of a friend of mine at the Longstone in the Isle of Wight (illustrated in my autobiography, *High Priestess*), which shows a similar beam of light issuing from the Longstone.

Stones *do* carry memories and can act as receptacles for any amount of unseen energies. It is not beyond the bounds of possibility that they also link on a psychic level with the ancient gods in whose names they were raised, and those people who erected them. By approaching a stone, touching it, and meditating upon its great age and its origins, you could receive an answer to a question. I know that this is true of the Whispering Knights at the Rollright complex. Many people have received messages from them – some form of guidance as to future events, and sometimes without even asking a question! If they have anything to tell you, it will flash into your mind, usually in the form of a rhyme. The words are very down-to-earth and very much to the point. I have received two communications from them, but on one occasion there was nothing but silence. Upon reflection, this was only a few months before my husband Arnold died, which surely indicates that they were reluctant to give bad news.

The Whispering Knights comprise of four 8-foot-high stones, which lean together, and a capstone which has fallen. They stand a quarter of a mile from the Circle on a natural rise within a field. It is thought that this monument was originally a burial chamber, and the story goes that it was once used by seers who prophesied from within its chamber. There is one stipulation for those who wish to communicate with the Whispering Knights: they must take a small cutting from an elder tree as an offering.

The subject of sacred sites brings to mind a wonderful verse about Avebury written by Edwyn, a High Priest of the Craft and a magical wordsmith, who has now entered the Summerlands. I include it here.

Directions

North of net's long barrow
the line lays easterly
to the wood henge circle centre
from the hill at Silbury.

Yet, to the west of Silbury,
south-west of Avebury,
south-west of the Cove is the Sacred Grove
on a hill, promontory.

In Avebury's centre circle;
The Cove stands on the sky,
a timeless portal centre we feel before we fly.

On the road that goes to Swindon
there stands the Goddess stone,
Blessed Be the Lady, the Maiden, Mother, Crone.

To the south, the stone to Belin
where Sun rays burn full flare,
The Sun-beams bright, branch out in flight
like antlers pierce the air.

The cycles all continue,
The seasons come and go.

In spite of change, we rearrange,
and start back where we go.

North of net's long barrow
the line lays easterly,
east and west, and north and south,
the centre sets us free.

What does the phrase 'the barrier between the quick and the dead' mean?

This is an old expression. The 'barrier' is the Magic Circle, and the 'quick' are the living, as opposed to the dead. The Magic Circle is considered to be 'between the worlds', hence the phrase was simply an old way of expressing the same thing: a Magic Circle, when erected, lies between the material and spiritual worlds.

Where did the 9-foot-diameter measurement for the size of the Magic Circle come from, Pat?

Most likely from the number nine which is the sacred number of the moon, and the number of moons it takes for a human child to be born. And undoubtedly it was found that a Circle 9 foot in diameter was the best size to accommodate thirteen witches most comfortably. Away from the Covenstead, however, the Circle can be of any size depending upon whether a witch is working alone, or with a partner, and according to the amount of space available.

In the old days there was also the important link with the nine maidens, three assigned to each of the three aspects of the Goddess – Virgin, Mother and Crone. These nine maidens also looked after the sacred fire of the Goddess, which was never allowed to go out: especially notable at the Temple of Vesta in Rome. The Path of the Hearth and Home is thought to be the most sacred of all the Paths. So the nine virginal maidens were allotted care of the fire in this way: three of them tended the fire; three fetched and prepared the fuel; while the remaining three virgins rested. An echo of this ancient rite is preserved in stone circles comprising of nine uprights and called 'The Nine Maidens'.

The measurements for a witch's Circle are also connected with the ancient and sacred form of measures now being overtaken in Britain by the idolatrous, false and atheistic metric system. This modern system was established in Paris in 1798, with a metre equal to 39.37 inches. Its chief claim to fame is that it corresponds with no existing or traditional unit of measure. It was designed by its inventors to be unlike any unit ever conceived to be convenient in actual use. The old sacred measure, when properly understood, promotes stability, harmony and knowledge, while the new system, brought forth in ignorance and conceit, is a suitable servant of the greedy forces of plutocracy currently in vogue. It has been introduced into Britain, but many commodities are labelled with both types of measurement, and items such as diaries include lists of weights and measures with both the old and the new units: a cunning way of presenting the new metric system because the majority of the British people would certainly reject it otherwise.

Stonehenge and other ancient structures were erected by use of the ancient measurements which included the megalithic yard, rediscovered and named by the late Professor Thom. These measurements relate to natural constants on more than one level and also demonstrate the unity between the macrocosm and the microcosm. As such, they have always been regarded as *sacred*. Of indefinable antiquity, they were known and used by ancient civilizations such as those of Sumer, Babylon, Chaldea and Egypt and still survive in parts of the world where the people are given precedence over the State. Happily, the USA still utilizes them and is determined to retain them.

Before the ancient measures were made into established units, some of them were originally conceived (as their names suggest) from the human form. An inch was gauged from the width of a carpenter's thumb; a builder estimated a 2-yard span by his outstretched arms; a surveyor paced by the yard; and a draper, up to recent times, measured fabric by the cubit – the distance from the elbow to the fingertip.

2 Of the Moon

Our lovely bright silver moon has been venerated throughout history as a symbol of the Goddess. It has inspired poets and artists and intrigued scientists as to how it came to be the Earth's satellite, controlling the tides of the oceans, gestation, and the growth of plants. On occult levels, its influence has been recorded in many diverse ways and it has been established as being a prime factor in affecting the minds and emotions of humanity.

Man's visit to the moon created a physical link with the orb which coincided, in astrological terms, with the Moon Cycle (1945 to 1981). The space adventure occurred *in this time frame*, a happening which gives much food for thought as to the influence of the moon, and the other celestial bodies, upon the Earth and its inhabitants. One major phenomenon in the Cycle of the Moon was of course the return of the Great Goddess!

What are the Mansions of the Moon? I have heard of them but never found a satisfactory explanation of them. Can you help, Patricia?

The Mansions of the Moon are the signs of the Zodiac which the moon travels through on its journeys around the world. And as the moon measures the entire Zodiac in a period of twenty-eight days, most of the ancient astrologers gave the time the moon spent in each sign the name 'Mansion', hence the 'Mansions of the Moon'. Doreen Valiente and I studied this subject and made a list of the various meanings of the signs when the moon illuminated them. We had some old papers with meanings which were written in archaic terminology, so we substituted a few for more modern expressions. I took note of them, with regard to meetings, and have reason to believe it aids a rite considerably if you choose a Mansion in tune with a rite.

Modern astronomers realize that the number twenty-eight is not an exact measurement of the orbital revolution of the moon, but it is close enough for our purposes. And for reasons based on magic, not science, the ancient people kept to this approximation, and also to a lunar rather than solar calendar.

The concept of the Mansions of the Moon is of very ancient origins reaching as far back as Suma, then to Babylon, Ancient Egypt, India, China and Arabia. It is known that great importance was given to the Mansions, and particular attention was paid to the one which held the full moon. We know that the Sumerians had a great civilization. They dug irrigation canals; developed a written language called cuneiform; and built the world's first cities. They also worshipped a trinity of gods: Nanna, a moon god who travelled among the stars in a crescent-shaped boat; Shamash, a sun goddess; and Ishtar – she of the morning star – Venus – who lived therein. As early as 3000 BC, the calendar of the Sumerians accurately predicted the changing of the four seasons.

The Babylonians followed closely on the heels of the Sumerians and probably absorbed some of their astrological knowledge. They were able to predict solar and lunar eclipses with startling accuracy. Ancient Egypt, too, had an immense knowledge of the heavens. They changed the Babylonian list of Mansions from seventeen to twenty-eight, in accordance with their magical beliefs about numbers, and systemized the twenty-eight constellations that stood in the path of the moon. They also combined them with their own zodiacal signs so that, by the second century AD, these lunar Mansions had been absorbed by zodiacal astrology.

The meanings of the diverse powers and virtues evoked by the moon in its wanderings through the twelve signs have been generally agreed upon by most of the ancient civilizations which have used them. There are also the moon's phases to be considered: whether in a given sign it is in a waxing or waning mode, at full, or dark, and especially if an eclipse is forthcoming. So, the meanings of the different Mansions have to be modified accordingly.

To make good use of the extra magical powers given by the Mansions of the Moon, you need a current ephemeris (astronomical almanac). This will give you the moon's position – the degrees, minutes and seconds of a particular sign of the Zodiac on every day and night of the year.

The Twenty-eight Mansions of the Moon

1. From 0°0 to 12°51'26" ARIES
A position of the moon for the making of pentacles for journeys and for working spells for love. It confers a great need for movement. It also facilitates comprehension. It symbolizes forces in conflict, whirlwinds – which are expressed in day-to-day life by quarrels. It exerts a very favourable influence on business. The fiery imagination.

2. From 12°51' 27" to 25°42' 52" ARIES
Time to make pentacles for the discovery of springs and treasures. It confers courage and also recklessness. Will and energy directed by thought not feeling. Luck, maternal love, triumph over illness. Determination in work. Unfavourable for sea journeys. Danger of rash actions.

3. From 25°42'53" ARIES to 8°34'18" TAURUS
For 'alchemical' experiments and for working spells of love and for sea journeys. Accentuates power of feelings. Great capacity for work. Good for sciences. Bad for marriage and travel by water. Good for thought processes, buying or selling, and travel by land.

4. 8°34′19″ to 21°25′44″ TAURUS

Working spells – diplomacy, work, small trade. Mental stability. Mostly a negative period. Bad for buildings. Marriage problems.

5. 21°25′45″ TAURUS to 4°17′10″ GEMINI

Helps return of a journey. Instruction of scholars. Health and goodwill. Spells for friendship and travel. Change of residence.

6. 4°17′11″ to 17°8′36″ GEMINI

Spells to give victory in conflict. Bad for farm work. Slows recovery after illness.

7. 17°8′37″ GEMINI to 0° CANCER

Influence on mental levels. Spells and pentacles for trade and luck in general and for favours from the great ones. Good for family life. Develops trust and friendship. Good for money matters, love affairs, planting and sowing. Bad for travel. Destroys authority.

8. 0° to 12°51′26″ CANCER

Good for children. Tenacity in action. Will-power set on certain goal. Good for social affairs – travellers – medical treatment. Drives away mice.

9. 12°51′27″ to 25°42′52″ CANCER

Prudence – tenacity – stability. Bad influence for travel.

10. 25°42′53″ CANCER to 8°34′18″ LEO

Spells/magic for love and buildings, benevolence and aid. Good for studies, earnings, professional success, love, social elevation. Good influence from a spiritual aspect.

11. 8°34′ 19″ to 21°25′44″ LEO

Good for trade and enables prisoners to escape! Good for marriage, travel, wealth, eloquence, actions with *clear* goals. Bad for taking purgatives.

12. 21°25'45" LEO to 4°17'10" VIRGO
Associated with the invisible world. Improves lot of prisoners, slaves and friends (includes all animals). Good for messages, love, happiness, knowledge, wealth through *personal* merit. Encourages study.

13. 4°17'11" to 17°8'36" VIRGO
Good for trade and crops. Good for travel – benevolence – gain. Sending of messages.

14. 17°8'37" VIRGO to 0° LIBRA
Spells for love, healing of sick. Blesses navigation. Increases happiness for leaders and teachers. Favours responsibility. Bad for journeys.

15. 0° to 12°51'26" LIBRA
Spells to hunt for springs and treasure and protect friends. Protects those in misfortune and distress. Bad for travel.

16. 12°51'27" to 25°42'52" LIBRA
Power of protecting oneself. Hinders marriage – travel – everything. Good for redemption of captives.

17. 25°42'53" LIBRA to 8°34'18" SCORPIO
Pentacles and spells for making people happy. Helps seamen, travel, charms for friendship and buildings.

18. 8°34'19" to 21°25'44" SCORPIO
Pentacles and spells for protection from enemies. Good for *exposing* enemies. Frees captives. Helps with buildings and secret operations.

19. 21°25'45" SCORPIO to 4°17'10" SAGITTARIUS
Pentacles and spells for luck in general, *but undertake nothing at this time.*

20. 4°17'11" to 17°8'36" SAGITTARIUS
Promotes eloquence and writings. Good for construction. Good influence for pentacles, spells and magic against witnesses. Compels a man to come to a certain place.

21. 17°8'37" SAGITTARIUS to 0° CAPRICORNUS
Pentacles, spells and magic to protect buildings, crops and money. Promotes travel, earnings and healing.

22. 0° to 12°51'26" CAPRICORNUS
Pentacles, spells and magic to stimulate healing. Brings friendship. Cures diseases. Helps captives, including animals, to escape.

23. 12°51'27" to 25°42'52" CAPRICORNUS
Beware of illnesses. Good for doctors and soldiers. Friendship with politicians. No engagements or contracts should be arranged.

24. 25°42'53" CAPRICORNUS to 8°34'18" AQUARIUS
Good for marriage plans, friendships, constructions. Confers knowledge with the star of fortune! This Mansion prevents laws being exercised. Travel by water is bad. Pentacles or talismans made now will be for trade or love, or to triumph over one's enemies.

25. 8°34'19" to 21°25'44" AQUARIUS
Protects messengers. Good for the effects of medicine.

26. 21°25'45" AQUARIUS to 4°17'10" PISCES
Pentacles for protection against dangers. Good for marriage, buying and selling, works of charity, medicine. Bad for ocean voyages.

27. 4°17'11" to 17°8'36" PISCES
Facilitates clairvoyance and psychic matters. Pentacles for fight-

ing illness. Charms for friendships. Good for meditations. Heals infirmities. Hinders builders. *Do not begin new projects.*

28. 17°8'37" PISCES to 0° ARIES

Pentacles for crops, business and conjugal affection. Increases merchandise and harvest. Protects travellers in dangerous or difficult places or circumstances. Bad for borrowing.

As will be seen from the above, the meanings are of ancient origin, but may be interpreted, in many cases, into present-day terminology. Much of the information concerning the Mansions of the Moon has been lost, which is why astrologers hardly ever mention them. However, I believe that nothing is ever completely lost, and knowledge can be recovered through divination. I think a study of the Mansions in this manner may be rewarding. The degrees of the Mansions should be charted and made into a star map, or even a list of them placed somewhere they will be noticed, and recalled when needed.

There is also a set of images for the Mansions of the Moon. These were included in Agrippa's work on occult philosophy and consist of twenty-eight magical seals. The images were to be designed during the time of a particular Mansion, when their influence and flow of power could be captured within the talisman, in the way that most talismans are usually made. The seals were then carried by the person for whom they were constructed, or put in the appropriate setting.

Here is the list of the twenty-eight images for encapsulating the power of each of the Mansions of the Moon.

1. The figure of a well-dressed woman, sitting in a chair with her right hand lifted up on her head. This is to be fumed with an incense of musk, camphor and calamus. The seal is to be set upon a silver square, set upon a silver ring.
2. The figure of a soldier sitting upon a horse, with a serpent in his right hand. This is to be fumed with an incense of red myrrh and storax. The image is set upon red wax.

3. The figure of the head of a man, set upon silver. This is fumed with an incense of red storax.

4. Upon white wax, the figures of two people embracing. This is fumed with an incense of aloes and amber.

5. Upon silver, the image of a well-dressed man, whose hands are raised in prayer. This is fumed with an incense of frankincense and myrrh.

6. Upon tin, the image of an eagle, with the face of a man. This is fumed with an incense of sulphur.

7. Upon lead, the image of a man holding his genitals in one hand and covering his eyes with the other. This is fumed with an incense of pine.

8. Upon gold, the head of a lion, fumed with amber.

9. Upon gold, the image of a man riding a lion. In his left hand he holds the lion's ear and in his right hand he extends a gold bracelet. This is fumed with an incense of myrrh, frankincense and saffron.

10. Upon blackened lead, the image of a dragon and a man in combat. This is fumed with some hairs from a great cat mixed in an incense of asafoetida.

11. Upon a white wax seal the image of a woman, and upon red wax the image of a man. These images are then pressed against each other so that the couple embrace. The seal is then fumed with an incense of aloes and amber.

12. Upon copper, the image of a dog biting its tail. This is then fumed with the smoke from burning some hairs from a black dog and cat.

13. The figure of a man who is sitting, writing letters. This is fumed with frankincense and nutmeg.

14. Upon silver, the image of a man sitting upon a chair with a balance scale in his hands. This is fumed with cinnamon.

15. Upon iron, the image of an ape. This is fumed with hair taken from an ape.

16. Upon copper, the image of a snake with its tail raised above its head. This is fumed with hartshorn.

17. Upon copper, the image of a woman holding her face with

both hands. This is perfumed with liquid storax.

18. Upon tin, the image of a male centaur. This is fumed with hair taken from a wolf.

19. The figure of a man with his own image behind and in front of him. This is fumed with sulphur and jet, then placed in a brass box along with your enemy's object link (hair, nails etc.) and some sulphur and jet.

20. Upon iron, the image of a man with winged feet and a helmet upon his head. This is fumed with argent vine.

21. Upon iron, the image of a cat with a dog's head. This is fumed with hair from a dog's head and buried where the destruction or decline is intended.

22. Upon iron, the image of a woman suckling her son. This iron seal is then heated to brand with. In herd animals the 'leader' is branded, usually upon the horn.

23. Upon a piece of fig wood, the image of a man planting. This is fumed with the flowers of a fig tree and hung in the area to preserve.

24. Upon white wax, the image of a woman brushing her hair. This is fumed with orris and coriander.

25. Upon red clay, the image of a winged man holding an empty vial. The seal is then mixed in with asafoetida and liquid storax, and burned. The burnt remains are then dropped into the body of water to be influenced.

26. Upon copper, the image of a fish. This is then fumed with the skin of a sea fish, and the seal is then tossed into the water you desire to fish.

27. Upon an iron ring, the image of a black man covered with hair and girdled the same, tossing a lance with his right hand. This is then sealed with black wax and perfumed with liquid storax while stating the desired effect.

28. Upon white wax (with mastic), the image of a crowned king. This is fumed with aloes.

3 Divination

Since time immemorial people have sought to know their future. Possibly the earliest form of divination was by water: gazing into a pool or pouring the liquid into a cauldron or bowl. In the latter method the water was usually consecrated by allowing the rays of a full moon to shine upon it. Pyromancy (divination by fire) was another way, but perhaps the most favoured method was by employing stones or even pebbles from the beach. The stones, by their shape or the symbols painted upon them, were held in the hands while the operator concentrated upon a question. Then the stones were released and scattered upon the ground, and by their positions the question would be answered.

Today, a popular *modus operandi* is the Tarot, and many hundreds of decks displaying different versions of these cards have been produced. They are ideal for long or short readings for single questions, or for an in-depth forecast covering several years.

I thought your verse on the Tarot, in The Tarot of the Old Path *(the book which accompanies the cards), was most evocative. Have you written any other poems on a similar theme, Patricia?*

I'm afraid not. But soon after I received your question, the unexpected happened! Or perhaps I should say in connection with the occult, the usual thing happened! A letter arrived from a friend of mine who enclosed a *poem on the Tarot* he had written and which he thought I might like. His name is Richard Middlebrook and he is a well-known Sheffield poet. Having received his permission, I include his masterly interpretation of the Tarot for your edification.

The Fool
Plants first in air
His footsteps limbo
Lost yet without care,
Only you make us grow.

The Magician
Elemental as childhood
Prestidigitation, fingers of light wood
All Fate's toys his play,
He is the light of Life's ray.

The Priestess
Veil. First universe,
Lonely was I
(Ego's hearse),
Carry me till I die.

The Empress
Pale queen of the black rock
Strong, defiant mother, pelican wise
All Life's threads shine in your summer frock;
All are rainbow children when you arise.

The Emperor
Guardian; sun ram of the flock,
The world slays you amid thorns
But you stand firm and your horns lock
And your fierceness oh ruddy king forever MORNS!

The High Priest
Bridge to castle of wise four
Mighty prime language you made

Yours was Man's first law
With Heaven's unruly sceptre you stand by Earth's door.

The Lovers
Married to day and night
Comes forth The Moment
When all are equal priests under the light
The lamp freely given by them to us; not pent.

The Chariot
Life's rugged road
The bent track is ours
Let Death be under the goad
And Life rejoice under heavenly choirs.

Strength
Lion of lust! Tamed by a silver hand,
First queen, priestess of the magical!
All that on earth you may understand;
Blossom of gold on the tree fantastical!

The Hermit
Your hand is your living, breathing, panting God
Thumb and fingers intuitively clasp
Rolling a philosophical stone through Subterrania's time-
    less abode;
You cling to Heaven with stubborn Eagle grasp.

Wheel of Fortune
Dead centre of the green mineralized universe
Millstone and hinge's grit, Age-end's infernal thrust
The breathing stone, the beating song and pulse of Life's
    verse
Life's very orb truculent amid machine dust.

Justice
Balancing the time's fury
The paths of ruin and glory.
ALL! Death! Fury! Law! Chaos!
Yours is the gift to give meaning to Life's story.

The Hanged Man
Flamed and lamed amid white threads
Mycelium gallow of moon-rise suspends
The Non-Thinking-Man in Thought's sheds;
Smilingly hangs up his hammock to Nights out there; Day ends.

Death
La Mort's whirling doom is the chariot against Life;
Cleansing, refreshing and ending stagnations.
Yours is the magic against mere mental strife,
You come to cut all men's sterile infatuations.

Temperance
Let silver and gold water's light
Sprinkle into Sun and Moon vases.
'stilled there in the temple of hallowed Night;
Let them temper all the virtues in their phases.

The Devil
Thrust power, Death in Life reborn,
Mortality's bane, sweet as Life.
Power be my pure God; thou unfettered horn!
Let me be always as a laughing devil 'mid vain
    philosopher's strife.

The Tower
Late Atlantean in pride
The one lidless eye of flame
Cracks full and wide
Leaving Time and Space orbs raining down far from blame.

The Star
In the sky's emptiness
Egypt first and last arose,
A star beside a pyramid to bless;
Through the desert a wind blows.

The Moon
Moon-ancient talisman, Death's ensign,
Unbreakable gateway except to the pure.
Silver labyrinths of lost cosmos deep in the Skies mine;
Before you shines your pride's narrow unlit way or its
    nettled cure.

The Sun
A garden of delight
Where full-grown adults play
Difficult to tell whether day or night
But The Sun is there in Life and Death's ray.

Judgement
The galaxy's centre stops
Men awake
This is the cream of the crops
The sky has become a giant cleansing rake.

The World
Purified The Sparks
Arise from silvery clothes;
Cast aside Earths and free as Larks
Sing free like Gods not wraiths.

4 What's in a Name?

Identification by means of a name is used throughout our vocabulary, and this is how it should be. Trouble arises when an object is given a name to conceal its real purpose, or a perfectly proper name is changed by improper usage to mean something different, such as the word 'occult'. This merely means 'hidden' – the sciences of the unseen such as telepathy, clairvoyance, clairaudience etc. In the Christian Church, however, its connotation has been altered to signify any kind of evil – black magic, devil worship, or some form of malignancy. And when a word or name is changed in this manner and is used often enough, it becomes identified in most people's minds with the false meaning. 'Witchcraft' is another such name.

Anything that is considered to be 'out of step' or in opposition to the establishment of the day is usually dealt with by this method. And, over a period of time, a word's false meaning will even enter dictionaries as its true definition.

Why was the Horned God called the Devil?

This occurred when the Christian Church became powerful and began to persecute witches. The Church was determined to eradicate the 'false' belief in the Old Gods one way or the other. Although there has never been a portrayal of the Christian Devil, in all the descriptions of him we are told that he has horns, a tail and cloven hoofs. In other words, they gave him the same attributes as the witch's Horned God, so that the witches' God would become identified with the Devil. The God of the Old Religion became the Devil of the new. This usually occurs when new religions come along and the old beliefs have to be banished from people's minds. And we must not forget the most beloved of the ancient gods, Pan, who had similar attributes, but because he belonged to the Greek pantheon of gods, whom the authorities preferred to the Celtic, he was generally ignored. As the god of shepherds and wild things, and with the ability to evoke the most exquisite music from his pipes, Pan had a special cave and altar at the foot of the Acropolis in Athens.

As time went on and prelates continued to fulminate against the Devil-worshipping witches, the witches themselves began to accept the term, too. This was most prevalent in Scotland. However, although Scottish witches may have called their god 'the Devill', they doubtless still knew him as the old Horned God.

This 'Devill' is said to have appeared at the witches' sabbats, and on occasions when more than one coven was assembled. He was usually dressed all in black and became known as the 'Man in Black', and more often than not his identity was unknown. This psychological aspect made sure that the witches had immediate respect for the stranger who stood before them in such a commanding position. Apart from Francis Stewart, Earl of Bothwell, the Master and leader of the North Berwick witches (who eventually escaped from the law and also from Scotland), the witch-hunters never caught the 'Man in Black'. There may be a very good reason for this. It never occurred to the witch-hunters that the 'Man in Black' could have been a woman! There was nothing to suggest it, and the voice would obviously have been disguised. From what I have learned over the years, I certainly believe this to be true; perhaps not in every case, but certainly in most.

Apropos the above, it is interesting to note that at the annual State Opening of the English Parliament, a member (usually a titled person), dressed entirely in black, summons the members of the House of Commons by knocking three times with the staff he carries upon the door leading to that House. His name is 'Black Rod' and he leads them to the House of Lords to hear the Queen's speech. Could this age-old authoritative custom have links with the 'Man in Black' once recognized by the witches?

Are the offices of the Maiden and the Summoner still used today?

The office of the Maiden certainly is: it is one of the most important positions in a coven. Besides assisting the High Priestess during the rituals, she is indispensable in being able to take over the role of the High Priestess in any emergency. The ancient working of the Triangle consists of the High Priestess, the High Priest and the Maiden. In Ancient Egypt this working involved Isis, Osiris and Nephthys – Nephthys being the sister of Isis.

Regarding the Summoner, this person was also indispensable in the old days for obvious reasons. As his name suggests, he (or she) summoned witches to a meeting by making the journeys, usually on horseback, to their homes. Today, there is really no need for a Summoner unless there are witches who have no telephones! Lastly, for the record and to correct a fallacy, the Sheffield coven did not have a 'Maiden' until 1970 when a Second Degree member achieved this title.

Is the title 'Queen of the Sabbat' still observed today?

It may well be, but for the benefit of my readers, this was a title given to a High Priestess, or a worthy female, to preside over an important sabbat or festival in the days prior to the persecutions, when such meetings were held with several covens taking part, even folk from the general population. It was an appellation given for the event, and most likely the well-known title 'Queen of the May' was taken from it. So it was an honour – a courtesy title – for a particular female who was considered to have earned it in some way.

The confessions of witches from court records mention meetings when three or four covens were present, and the *Royne du*

Sabbat sat at the Master's left hand during the feast. It is also made clear that this 'Queen of the Sabbat' was only a figurehead – as the witch Isobel Gowdie stated at her trial in 1662 – while the Maiden of the coven was present at every meeting.

This fact is acknowledged by Dr Margaret Murray, in *The Witch-Cult in Western Europe*. From this book we see that in Scotland in the seventeenth century a witch known as the Maiden of the Coven held an important position; and in other places, another woman, not the queen, had the highest status, next to the Grand Master. This other woman was obviously the High Priestess.

Many years ago, a lady from Glasgow wrote to me and told me that her grandam was Queen of the Sabbat on the island of Tiree for many years, and that her grandam gave her magical tools to the lady's mother who still used her craft for different purposes, and also for solo workings. Her grandam, she said, always maintained that those people who are meant to be taught and initiated find the way. Tiree is a small island in the Outer Hebrides, and even today is regarded as semi-archaic. The writer also mentioned that the Athame and Cup had belonged to her great-great-grandam, who had passed them down, together with a Pentagram-inlaid book support. Her letter contained the affirmation: 'Great is the mother that giveth all, as Thy laws are, so shall be!'

Gerald Gardner once performed a ritual in which he gave me the courtesy title 'Queen of the Sabbat', and made me a special silver crown for the occasion. As a High Priest and Elder of the Craft, he had the authority to bestow this honour, and evidently thought I was worthy of it. Be that as it may, the idea of a silver crown caught on and became the accoutrement of many present-day High Priestesses.

How do you feel about the term 'Wicca'? Should we stick with 'Witchcraft', and if not, why not?

I don't know how we can stick with the name 'Witchcraft' when most adherents have already changed it to 'Wicca'! I think the latter is an OK term, but from the 1950s it was the name 'Witchcraft' which fired the public's imagination and aided the renaissance of the Craft.

Most Christians will always give the word 'Witchcraft' a negative bias, although Germanic sources state that it belongs to a group of words whose underlying sense means 'set apart as sacred', and 'one having the power to make sacred'. On the surface, 'Wicca' is a more 'respectable' name than 'Witchcraft', but it does not carry the integrity of the latter.

5 Herbs and Flowers

In most people's minds, and even in some modern witches' ones too, witches of old are seen as being part of a rural community and skilled in the art of healing through their knowledge of herbalism. Certainly, the village wise woman was the National Health Service of her time. She was also consulted when magic spells were required, benign or otherwise: in fact all manner of troubles and ailments were brought to her door to be resolved.

However, not all witches were of this variety. There were those who belonged to the Priesthood of the Craft, and many adherents who held prominent positions in life. Historical accounts reveal that various royal personages were also involved in witchcraft. The emphasis here would be much more on the working of magic and ritual than upon the virtue and usage of plants, although certain ancient spells involving particular herbs were a part of the Priesthood's hidden knowledge and were handed down through the years.

Young ladies of distinction and good breeding were often coached in witchcraft by a female member of the household staff: someone who was the young lady's maid and also her confidante. The Craft was often passed down in unusual ways, but passed down it certainly was!

Do you know anything about the language of flowers? I believe much of it has been lost today.

I have some knowledge of this subject, gleaned from a rare booklet I bought many years ago at an antique fair. Gerald Gardner knew quite a lot about certain flowers and plants that witches used in their herbal cures and spells, including some which were poisonous and incorporated into mixtures which were rubbed into certain parts of the body to induce travelling in the Astral realms.

However, in the Victorian era most people knew a little about what certain flowers stood for; usually these were popular flowers like roses and lilies, and the ones which were sent on special occasions. But lovers in earlier times knew that each flower had a meaning; we know this because books were written on the subject and girls often carried small pocket editions around with them. A friend of mine had one that was sent to a Miss Clark by an admirer in 1868.

Today, most men when they buy flowers for a lady grab the first bunch the flower-seller offers them, in a rather embarrassed manner, or ring the florist and ask them to make one up. But by no means all men act in this way. Some choose a bouquet very carefully, although they probably have no idea what the flowers mean. If they did, they would be looked upon as relics of Victorian sentimentality. However, the sugary verses in modern greeting cards show that we are still as sentimental as our forebears although, now that money has become a god, a man's affections (or even a woman's) are often judged by the cost of the presents they give.

The love-sick maiden of long ago thought more of a posy of wild flowers than any hothouse blooms, provided they conveyed the proper sentiments. These silent messages of love could be gathered in woods or meadows. The exotic blossoms of recent years have no place in the flower vocabulary.

The rose has always stood for love and beauty and holds a special magical place in many esoteric societies. It was immortalized by Robert Burns in his poem 'My love is like a red, red rose'. The meanings vary according to the type of rose. A red rose-bud means you are young and beautiful, while one in full flower means beauty only. A white rose-bud signifies a heart ignorant of love, but one in full bloom says 'I am worthy of you'. Two white buds added to the latter shows the sender is faithful to a secret entrusted. The lover who sends a Christmas rose is asking his desired-one to tranquillize his anxiety, and an Austrian rose tells her that she is all that is lovely.

One can imagine a young girl finding a nosegay of mixed flowers from someone, running to her bedroom and proceeding to decode all the meanings with the help of her little book of flower language that she kept hidden in a secret drawer. She may have discovered that her admirer proclaimed his gallantry by sending a sweet-william; a speedwell asked if she would be faithful; while a violet assured her that he would be so for ever. A wallflower in the nosegay added that his fidelity would continue, even in misfortune. Strawberry leaves showed his esteem and love, and a white poppy informed her how he dreamed of her at night. A pansy said that she occupied his thoughts during the day too. Even a piece of straw that bound the flowers together signified a union and his desire to make her his wife.

The girl could reply by leaving some flowers where she had found his, the meanings of which could make him full of hope, or destroy his dreams for the future. A pasqueflower anemone meant, 'You have no claims on me', and a sprig of gorse would show her anger at his impertinence. If he did receive such 'messages', he might leave a stem of hemlock that said her refusal of him would lead to his death. He hoped that this would change her mind. If she only accepted his platonic friendship, he would be satisfied. This she could convey by leaving him a sprig of acacia.

Flower language was not only used by those in love; it could communicate warnings – messages of illness or even approaching death. The receiver of bay leaves would quickly realize that the sender, or one of their near relatives, was about to pass over. Field anemone showed that the sender was sick, and marigolds that they were in pain. The outbreak of war was indicated by milfoil, and victory by palm. The receiving of bilberry warned against treachery, while whortleberry denoted treason. Bittersweet nightshade stood for truth.

The witches of old used flower language to warn other

41

witches or covens of forthcoming dangers, especially during the time of the persecutions. A few examples will reveal how simple this method of passing secret information could be. If a witch found some dead leaves piled up on her doorstep, she would know that some sadness had befallen the Craft. It usually meant that one of the members had been caught, or that the witchfinders had arrived in the town or village. Stinging nettles left near the door revealed that some scandal was being spread about concerning the receiver. And a piece of cedarwood left on a window-sill suggested that the witch should keep up her strength and all would be well. It seemed that the position of these 'messages' was very important, too. If they were left on the doorstep, the news was not good; but if on a window-sill there was not too much to worry about. If they were on a nearby bush or tree, it would indicate that the 'message' concerned some future event – a celebration, a birth, or a Handfasting. Garden marigolds foretold some uneasiness in the local coven, and a pile of grass informed the local witches to unite against a common enemy.

When a new person applied to join the Craft, they were always interviewed twice; first by a member of a coven, who then sent them to be vetted by a High Priest or Priestess. The candidate was always given some flowers to take to their second examiner. Little did they know that the flowers conveyed information about themselves! The following list will give some indication of how flower language was used to give a coven leader some initial idea about the character of the person they were to interview.

African marigolds implied that the candidate was vulgar-minded, but a sprig of mint added to them showed that there was a certain amount of virtue. Mulberry leaves meant wisdom, but meadowsweet signified that the first witch considered the candidate to be useless. One who was thought to be insincere or dangerous was given foxgloves, while vine leaves told the leader that the person was prone to drunkenness. Thyme conveyed the fact that they were mean, and narcissus flowers revealed that the candidate was very self-centred. Fern, however, denoted sincerity. Several flowers and herbs were often combined together, to give a broad outline of a person's character.

It is not to be assumed that the above tests automatically granted a candidate initiation, but it certainly saved time and energy if a person was totally unsuitable. We know that flowers bloom at different times of the year, which is why the witches dried many of them and kept them for the purposes thus described. And flower language was so extensive that particular meanings could always be contrived, or arrived at, by one plant or another.

Although the use of flowers and herbs to send messages has largely been replaced by the telephone and postal services, not to mention email, during the Second World War, members of the underground movement in occupied areas often used this method to send warnings and secret information back to London.

Witches often use various magical plants in their spells; do you know of any unusual ones?

I have plenty of the favourite ones growing in my garden, including Solomon's-seal. This is a very magical plant and one not too well known. It has been highly praised throughout the ages for its magical powers. A beautiful plant, it has rounded arching stems, with hanging greenish-white, bell-shaped flowers. Its elliptical leaves are a shiny dark-green and its fruit is in the form of a small black berry. Most unusual. Its magical powers, however, reside in the root, which when cut displays a perfect six-pointed star. This most potent and naturally occurring sigil may have been used by the great magician, Solomon, hence the name, but its origins are far older and lost in the mists of time. Medicinally, the plant's root is good for rheumatism: it is mashed and applied to the joint in question. Plants have been given an astrological link and a corresponding planetary ruler. Solomon's-seal is owned by Saturn.

The fern is perhaps a plant which gains little attention. Many legends have been woven around it and most of them give it a dark, uncanny influence. The variety known as *Aspidium flixmas*, or 'lucky hands', flowers only once, and then at night. It is said to be very lucky to see the dark-red blossoms open, but only on St John's Night (24 June). The really precious part is the seed, which may be seen shining like molten gold in the darkness. If you scatter it while making a wish that the treasures of the earth be revealed, you may see them in a ghostly blue light, as if the earth were glass. Indeed, glass made from this fern's ashes is said to have mysterious properties. The ring of Genghis was supposed to have been made this way and brought to its owner comprehension of the speech of birds.

The trailing cinquefoil or five-leafed flower is said to confer power upon all who carry it. Its leaves, shaped like a hand, are believed to help obtain favours and make the possessor clever! Jupiter rules it, and the witches of old used it to heal a variety of ills. A very useful plant. I must mention the iris or *fleur-de-lys*, the flower of Louis, which confers inspiration. Witches have long used this plant in their love spells. A most beautiful flower, too. It has been incorporated in many coats of arms, being of a unique shape and of an exquisite blue colour. The root provides the famous orris powder, or face powder but, as a magical plant for provoking love, it is said to be one of the best. Its ruler is the Moon.

There are a great many flowers and plants which have been used in the belief that their influences will attract love, and most of them are ruled by Venus. These include lad's love or southernwood, love-in-a-mist, vervain, elecampane, clover, yarrow and coriander: the list is almost endless. Myrtle too must be included here. It is sacred to the goddess Aphrodite and therefore has always been associated with love. Under the rulership of Mercury, it is a lovely bush to have in your garden. In August, small, white posies of flowers appear – very pretty. The plant's uses are many and varied. In homeopathy it is used for many different ailments, while the fragrant flowers are a constituent of toilet water and dried in pot-pourri and herb pillows. The buds and berries are often incorporated in sweets. For a swift reply to a letter, rub it with myrtle leaves.

The magical and mystical virtue hidden in plant life is known to country folk as 'wortcunning'. Plants have been studied down the ages by witches and those in touch with nature, and they have become associated with both positive and negative magic. In olden times, incantations and prayers would be recited over a plant before using it. This was done for a number of reasons, the principal one (which still holds good today) was that, being a living thing, a plant had its own spirit and life force, and would therefore respond to a person's wishes more easily if addressed in this way.

A very solemn incantation to a plant was spoken by Greek physicians of Alexandria:

Thou wert sown by Cronos, made welcome by Hera, protected by Ammon, born of Isis, nourished by Zeus of the rains. Thou hast grown by favour of the Sun and of the dew. Thou art the dew of all the gods. The heart of Hermes, the seed of the high gods, the eye of the Sun, the light of the Moon, the dignity of Osiris, the beauty and the glory of the sky, the soul of the demon of Osiris, who feasts in all places, the breath of Ammon. Rise up, as thou hast caused Osiris to rise up, lift thyself up like the Sun. Thou art tall as the zenith; thy roots are deep also as the abyss. Thy virtues are in the heart of Hermes; thy branches are the bones of Mnevis; thy flowers, the eye of Horus; thy seeds, the seed of Pan. I purify thee with resin even as the gods, for my good health; be purified also by my prayer and be powerful, for our sake, as Ares or Athene. I am Hermes. I pick you with good luck, and with the Good Demon, and at the propitious hour, on the day which is right and propitious for all things.

What plant would not prove strong and potent with such eloquence and spiritual fervour?

In the days of Queen Elizabeth I, a confection known as

'Kissing Comfits' was very popular. These were made from eryngo roots (sea holly), and mixed with sugar. Sea holly had the reputation of being an aphrodisiac – hence the name! These sweets were revived in the seventeenth century by an apothecary named Burton, who opened a factory at Colchester specifically for this purpose.

Certain plants have always been used by witches in the art of divination and clairvoyance. Rue is one of these as it is associated with the Moon Goddess. A little of the dried herb is burned as an incense during these activities. Rue does in fact make the eyes keener and the mind more alert but must be used with great discretion. Fumes of linseed, roots of violets and parsley are also said to be conducive to prophesying. Mugwort is often employed in the consecration of a scrying instrument, the speculum being smeared with its juice.

Many witches, including me, grow a moon plant in their gardens or window-boxes, in honour of both the Goddess and the Moon. They are white, sweet-smelling flowers or plants with a moon signature such as senna and moonwort. A really beautiful one is lunary, or honesty, sometimes called white satin. The lovely deep-mauve flowers give way to the three-fold septa which carry the seeds. These are moons exactly, being moon-coloured, translucent and shiny. Their beauty as an indoor decoration is well known. And thus with this plant, the Goddess and the Moon can be honoured both indoors and out.

What herbs or plants can be used for banishing negative influences?

Many herbs are said to banish negative influences and give protection from these nasty vibrations. They were certainly used in the olden days, and I suspect were added to spells by way of fumigations or incense. They were also made into sachets to wear as an addition to a spell.

Cleansing your home of negative influences is quite an easy operation. Halve some onions and place a cut half in every room, hallway and flight of stairs. After seven days, replace them with fresh onions until you feel a definite and positive change has occurred. Throw all the used onions away after use. They will have absorbed all the negativity. Burning them immediately would be best.

Incense made from myrrh or frankincense is extremely powerful and beneficial to burn when suffering from depression or bad luck. And the bulb of a flowering daffodil is said to put evil to flight. A wild one is best, but a garden daffodil will do. This flower was originally called asphodelus and affodilus, names which evolved into its present one. According to Greek mythology, it grew in the meadows of the Underworld, and so it has a definite occult significance. Dig up the bulb and cut off the flower head; this can be saved in some water. Wash the bulb well, then wrap it in a clean white cloth and carry it with you, or hang it up in your home. Venus governs white daffodils and Mars the yellow ones.

Cinquefoil, which as its name suggests, has five leaflets, is somewhat like a hand. If carried on the person it is said to bestow a sharper mind and help in obtaining favours. Culpeper, the seventeenth-century herbalist and astrologer, cannot speak highly enough of this herb as, apart from any mystical qualities, it can cure so many ills, pains and aches. Cinquefoil is under Jupiter.

Fennel is an old favourite for warding off evil, and mugwort – the 'traveller's herb' – protects a person from unfriendly spirits during a journey. Garlic flowers, if worn, need no explanation; they may even rid you of your friends! True laurel, or sweet bay, is considered the king of herbs. Used to crown the victor in ancient times, it has countless virtues for protection. Pick St John's wort on Midsummer Day (24 June). It has magical properties for luck and love and, according to the witches of old, will drive away evil of any kind. Dry it and keep it in a little bag about your person. This plant, with its bright yellow flowers, is under the dominion of the sun.

A number of these herbs can be blended together in a sachet if their rulers are in harmony, but make sure the ones you choose add up to an odd number. Odd numbers are said to be pleasing to the Gods. Protective colours for sachets are: white, for dispelling bad influences; blue, for occult protection; and purple, for power in overcoming negative forces.

A traditional magical tree is the rowan or mountain ash. The old method for protection by this tree is as follows. Take two small twigs from a rowan tree (after first requesting the spirit of the tree for this favour). Then, using red thread, bind them together in the form of a cross which, when turned through forty-five degrees, becomes the Geofu or Gebu rune – the one used (perhaps unknowingly) when you put kisses on a letter. This rune means a gift or a blessing. You must then hang the cross on some red ribbon and place it around the neck of whomever the spell is for, with the following words:

> About thy neck this cross I place,
> cross of quickbeam, cross of grace;
> may it safely guard thy way
> and keep thee safely night and day.

I must include what I consider to be the overlord of protective herbs and plants. This is the mandragore or root of the mandrake. *Mandragora officinalis* which belongs to the species Solanaceae is extremely poisonous if consumed but, as this particular counter-magic has nothing to do with a cooking recipe, I mention that only as a warning. The infamous mandrake comes from the eastern Mediterranean and is a costly and rare plant, so occultists use in its place the English mandrake or white bryony which is just as traditional. It must be realized, however, that it is now illegal to dig up wild plants without the landowner's permission. Assuming this has been given, here is the method of preparation.

On a day of the waxing moon, a few days after the new moon, and in the 'Dark Tide', sometime between the winter solstice and the spring equinox, search for your mandrake in hedgerows and well-drained soil. When you have located the plant and verified it with appropriate sources, make sure you know its exact position as you must return to the same spot after dark to dig it up.

You are required to perform this act alone, so when you are sure no one is in the vicinity, take a longish sharp knife, or similar implement, and proceed to loosen the earth around the plant's root. The root is what you want, so be as careful as you can not to injure it in any way. Clear the earth well away from the root with a suitable tool, then gently draw the plant from the soil. You may have to pull quite hard at first, and of course there is the legend that when the plant is dragged from the earth it groans!

Trim all the foliage off the plant's main stem and cut the root from it, also a small piece from near the bottom of the stem. This you should bury in the hole from which the plant was drawn, and cover up. Take the major part of the root home and clean it with milk. Next, you must decide whether the shape of the root looks to be male or female, as these roots are nearly always divided into a number of smaller ones. The mandrake has to be of the sex opposite to your own, so, with a knife (if you are a witch, the white-handled knife), proceed to make any suitable adjustments to it, but accentuating rather than destroying the root's salient features. Carve the semblance of a face upon it – this also is important. During this activity, repeatedly chant a short phrase, for whatever kind of protection you desire.

On an evening of your choice, bury this root in either a churchyard, or where two paths meet or cross. This would give the maximum efficacy but, if neither of these places is possible, choose a spot convenient to you. Then, for the next month, twenty-eight days from the time you first dug it up – you must water the place regularly. Some occultists use distilled water and milk mixed together; the water however should predominate, with nine parts to three of milk.

The lunar month at an end and the hour fast approaching midnight, it is time to dig your root up again so, using the same implement that you employed originally, unearth the root for the last time. You may discover that the carvings you made on the figure have healed over and that it looks more like an actual manikin. After cleaning the root of any loose earth, dry it as thoroughly and *naturally* as possible. This will take time; usually about three or four months, depending on where you put it to dry. An airing cupboard above a hot-water tank, or where warm air constantly rises, would be ideal. Don't forget either that the mandrake should not be shown to all and sundry; the more secret you keep it, the better. Finally, it should be passed through the smoke of vervain leaves every day during the drying period, and then put into a box lined with vervain leaves, where it will live when not being used or handled. Keep the box near to your hearth and in the room you most frequently inhabit. Replace the vervain leaves from time to time.

This magical manikin can be used for all kinds of protection and luck. Tell it what you require, and treat it lovingly. And if the time comes when you can no longer care for it, you may pass it to another witch or occultist of the same sex as yourself, who you know will understand its potency.

Do you think plants feel pain like us, Pat? Are they capable of feelings?

I am not an expert in this field, but plants are sentient and are definitely living things. Their awareness must be at a level of consciousness commensurate with their position in the kingdom of vegetation. This is much lower than that of humans, animals and birds in that they do not appear, among other attributes, to have brains. Nervous systems link to brains in order that messages to the body can be given and received. These messages can also include those of pain and inform the brain that something is wrong with a certain part of the body. Now, if plants have no brains, they may have a different method of 'knowing'. One thing is certain, plants *do* respond to loving care and attention. Laboratory experiments have been taking place for some time, mostly in the interests of agriculture, and this much has been proved. In the Old Religion it has always been known that plant-life, and indeed all vegetation, has a 'knowing' of its own, which is why festivals and folk-rituals are still perpetuated in order to thank Mother Nature for all her gifts.

Everything that lives is part of a vast, intricate and correlated pattern, not merely a material one but a spiritual one also. Sensitive people and those with deeper perceptions than the average body-consciousness of most humans, have a closer affinity with plants and have observed how they appear to react to human vibrations and touch. A dear friend of mine, who passed over some years ago, told me that one morning while in her garden she noticed a little blue flower which she had not previously seen. As she gazed at it, a lovely blue light slowly appeared around it and enclosed the flower within it. My friend was unable to take her eyes from the sight, but eventually ran indoors to fetch her husband to see it. Alas, when she returned to the garden, accompanied by her spouse, the ethereal light had gone. Obviously, the vision was meant for her alone.

It is bewildering to think of the millions of different plants and flowers in the world, and how dissimilar they are from each other. Then, there are plants that are used in healing a multitude of ills, and others which are extremely poisonous, although many of the latter, when blended with other ingredients, become beneficial in present-day pharmacology. There are also plants which actively dislike others and, if planted near them, will shrivel up and die. Gardeners have learned much of this lore, but do not know why this should be so. It would certainly be an intriguing subject to study.

All this brings to mind Kirlian photography. This was discovered by Semyor Kirlian, a Russian electrician, in 1939. He began experimenting with objects placed in a high frequency electrical field, and accidentally photographed his own hand while thus engaged. The result was quite amazing, as the picture showed a mystifying glow emanating from the tips of his fingers. Leaves were found to give the same results, revealing a similar energy field; and when a leaf was cut in half, *the energy field of the missing piece was still there.* This astonishing phenomenon came to be known as the phantom leaf effect.

It appears to me that what this light depicts is the astral body of the leaf. If this is true, it could mean that everything that is has its astral counterpart and exists upon the Astral Plane.

6 Astrology

Cynics and sceptics may deride the science of astrology but they cannot deny the fact that the Earth and the small group of planets which circle our Sun are, in terms of galactic space, in close proximity to each other. Therefore, in terms of vibration, the planets, as well as the Sun and the Moon, undoubtedly have an influence upon the Earth – the only planet (as far as we are aware) in our little 'family' to engender human life.

The Star Map showing the positions of the Sun, Moon and planets at an individual's birth reveals their life pattern. This knowledge has been gleaned by observation over thousands of years. Many men of genius were supporters of astrology – Aristotle, Francis Bacon, Spinoza, Schiller, Byron, Emerson, Shelley, Napoleon and Goethe spring to mind. The greatest scientists and astronomers of the ages, including Galileo and Sir Isaac Newton, were also astrologers. And this ancient science, the mother of astronomy, is one of the fundamental concepts of the Old Religion.

In ancient times, people regarded the Zodiac as the 'Wheel of Necessity' or the 'Wheel of Fate', but it must be emphasized that 'the stars impel – they do not compel'. Plotinus taught that 'The circuit of the stars indicates definite events to come but without being the direct cause of what happens'. Pythagoras asserted, 'Revolving around the "Wheel of Necessity", the psyche is transformed and confined at different times in different bodies.'

Patricia, how important is the knowledge of astrology to Craft rituals?

Extremely important, because the Eight Ritual Occasions are based on the time of the year and on the signs of the Zodiac. Although witches know when a major festival occurs, it is also imperative to know the *sign* of the Zodiac in which the festival is set. Why? Because the sign informs you about the nature of the festival and what type of cosmic energy is manifesting at that time of the year. A thorough knowledge of the signs of the Zodiac is necessary for any witch who is studying the Mysteries. Equally important is to become *au fait* with your own birth chart in order to discover your true character and why you have been born (or reborn) at this time.

The Zodiac reveals the pattern of the year and should be as familiar to an adherent as their own names. They should also have an ephemeris which gives the movements of the Sun, Moon and planets throughout the year. At the very least, you need to have an understanding of the Four Tides of the year, as these reveal the most favourable times for the working of particular forms of magic.

The Moon is the prime mover for working magic upon Astral levels, and this type of magic is the one most used in the Craft. Witches and occultists always consult an ephemeris or a diary to find a phase of the Moon which is most suitable for a ritual they intend to perform. The signs it will travel through during a particular phase is also crucial – finding which one is most conducive to the ritual. The Moon's tremendous influence and power upon the Earth has long been recognized, on both material and ethereal levels; it is literally the *power* of growth and is known as 'the Increaser'.

Power arises in space; it is taken by the Sun and transmitted to the planets in its family. The planets pass it on, each one with its own particular vibration. This is the basis of astrology. I think of the Moon as the nurse of the Earth – the feminine orb – and the fact that there was once a lunar calendar illustrating the thirteen full moons in a year (only very occasionally are there just twelve) indicates the sacredness in which the Moon, and indeed the number thirteen, was once held. Of course, to fishermen and others who go to sea, the phases of the Moon are as familiar as the backs of their hands. The Moon governs the tides and each day there are two high tides, so the times when these occur have to be calculated and publicly displayed in harbours for the benefit of sea-going vessels.

Except in Qabalistic symbology, the Moon is thought of as feminine and is a symbol of the Goddess. Much ancient art depicts the Goddess wearing the horns of the new moon upon Her head. An early lunar ritual from Greece, in which priestesses of the Moon draw down its power into a pool or mirror, is pictured upon a Greek vase c.200 BC. Gerald Gardner made a sketch of it and named it 'Drawing Down the Moon'. The picture is very intriguing and bears a striking similarity to the way witches work today. Two naked female witches stand with an arm extended to the Moon. One holds a short sword, or knife; the other, what looks very much like a wand. One of the witches wears a cap, the other is bareheaded, and they are both portrayed as very comely. The Moon is full with the face of the Goddess looking down upon the participants of the rite from within it. And from the Moon a stream or spiral of what could be lunar fluid or energy issues and falls on to the ground between the two women. This ancient rite was evidently considered important enough and well-known enough to be etched upon a vase. The other explanation, of course, is that the vase was a one-off, and painted by a high priestess for her own personal use. We shall never know!

In your book The Zodiac Experience *and the visualization in the Rite of Cancer, why is Noah associated with the 'Ark of a thousand years'?*

I am so pleased that you asked this question. Over the years, I had forgotten about this error but, when the book was reprinted by Capall Bann, I made a point of drawing the publisher's attention to it, so that finally it was printed correctly. 'Noah' should read

'Nuah', which was an ancient name of the Goddess in the Middle East. When the book was first published by Samuel Weiser, corrections were made as usual by the then editor, but no mention was made of the name 'Nuah'. However, when the book was published the name had been changed to 'Noah'! Whether the editor saw it, thought it was an error, and changed it to a name that she knew, or whether it was the 'printer's devil', I shall never know, but it was a big disappointment to me. And I was of the opinion that readers would think I had gone loopy in bringing old Noah into the Mother's 'Moon Boat'. But this shows how names can be altered to procure a totally different character, and how those who wrote the Old Testament did in fact change a name of the Goddess into that of an old man called Noah, and built around him the legend of the Ark, together with male and female pairs of every animal and bird that existed upon the Earth.

The Ark is the shape of the female oval, the *vesica piscis*, which has long been recognized as the shape of the vagina, out of which comes all life. This oval shape is incorporated in many art-forms, especially in medieval religious paintings of the Virgin and Child where Mary is sitting within it. (Yet another example of a 'borrowing' from the Old Religion.)

The symbol of the *vesica piscis* is made from two interlaced circles, and a most beautiful one in fine wrought ironwork can be seen on the cover of Chalice Well in Glastonbury. The cover itself is made of Somerset oak to protect the wonderful well-chamber from contamination.

John Michell, in his invaluable book, *The View over Atlantis*, tells us that although Stonehenge was built upon the magical square of the Sun, the mystical *vesica piscis* forms the foundation of the entire structure. Further, he states that the *vesica* lies under every great temple of antiquity, and even those of early Christianity. Michell quotes Dr Oliver from *The Canon*, who says:

This mysterious figure Vesica Piscis possessed an unbounded influence on the details of sacred architecture; and *it constituted the great and enduring secret of our ancient brethren*. The plans of religious buildings were determined by its use; and the proportions of length and height were dependent on it alone.

Are you familiar with the thirteenth sign of the Zodiac – Arachne? And what does it mean if a planet in your natal chart falls in that sign?

Yes, I am familiar with Arachne but, for readers who are not, I will explain the basics of the thirteenth sign.

There was once a lunar year of thirteen full moons, and there was also a zodiac of thirteen signs. But this thirteenth sign was dropped when the changeover from a lunar to a solar year occurred.

Arachne was depicted, as the name suggests, as a spider goddess, and thousands of artefacts have been found all over the world with a spider engraved upon them. The story of Arachne is one of the Greek legends and is related to the Zodiac. Arachne was originally a woman and a skilled weaver of tapestries, but Athena, the strong and powerful goddess of war, the arts and learning, became jealous of Arachne's skill and challenged her to a duel. This duel involved each of them weaving a lovely but complex picture, and the gods were asked to judge between them. The prize was given to Arachne, and Athena became so enraged that she changed Arachne into a spider. Despairing of life, Arachne hanged herself. This act accounts for a spider dangling on its own thread.

Where does Arachne fit into the present Zodiac? And where was her proper place as the thirteenth sign? James Vogh gives a brilliant analysis of this problem in his book, *The Thirteenth Zodiac – The Sign of Arachne*. I urge you to read it. The clues have much to do with names and threads. For example, Arianrhod, the Lady of the Silver Wheel, is said to be another name for Arachne. The Cretans called Arachne Ariadne, meaning 'spinner'. Ariadne had a ball of thread to guide Theseus out of the Labyrinth after he had killed the Minotaur. Now, the Minotaur's actual name was Asterion ('of the stars') so how did it come to be known as the Minotaur?

Robert Graves in *The Greek Myths* says the name Minos is astrological and means 'the Moon's creature'. This is where Vogh asks, '. . . if the entire legend could not be an allegory explaining the location of the thirteenth sign? Could it fall between the Twins and the Bull?' His reasoning depends upon the Minotaur being half-bull, and Theseus having a twin brother, Peirithous. The Minotaur therefore is half of the sign of the Bull, while Theseus is half of the sign of the Twins, with the spider-thread of Ariadne connecting them. So, we now look at the constellations in this part of the sky: Ge*mini* + *Tauru*s = *Min(o)taur.*

Graves says, 'Numerous seals with a spider emblem have been found at Cretan Miletus', and he asserts that the spider cult was linked to the Cretan trade of spinning and weaving. In Vogh's book, there are many more links between the Zodiac and the spider goddess which are equally fascinating and convincing.

The Sun enters the sign of the Spider on 16 May and leaves it on 13 June. Astrologer A.R. Ramsden called the people who were born between these dates 'Araneans', and considered that they had a greater chance of being psychic than those born in other signs of the Zodiac. Even if they are not psychic, they are 'special' people, vibrantly alive and energetic, yet often haunted by thoughts of death. Araneans can be poets or musicians, they may have extraordinary singing or speaking voices, and they are skilful in one-to-one communication. Politics or drama, it matters not what they pursue, as they have an inborn talent for *influencing* people. This is the key to the Aranean personality, but it is always combined with *sympathy*.

In the regular or tropical Zodiac, it is simple to calculate the position of Arachne. The critical area lies between 25°23′ of Taurus, and 23°5′ of Gemini. A psychic person born with the Sun, Moon or Ascendant in Arachne is considered to be a psychic Aranean. Other psychics, while not having this configuration in their natal charts, may yet have some other planet in Arachne, which gives them a special gift of one kind or another. As to the ancient symbol for Arachne, this is an equal-armed cross within a circle. In the past this symbol has been adopted in different parts of the world for many diverse reasons, both mystical and magical and, of course, by those who knew the Spider Goddess.

In medieval times, the symbol was rejuvenated in horoscopes to become something called 'The Part of Fortune'. It is the only segment used by astrologers. 'The Part of Fortune' is regarded as the Good Genius of the horoscope, but is derived from entirely different calculations than those of Arachne, the thirteenth *sign* of the Zodiac. Therefore, apart from having the same symbol, 'The Part of Fortune' has nothing to do with Arachne, the sign of the Spider Goddess.

7 Gerald Brosseau Gardner

Having written so much myself about Gerald over the years, I would like here to give the honour of doing so to an associate of his, James Laver CBE, Hon. RE, FRSA, FRSL, who for a long period was Keeper of the Prints and Drawings at the Victoria and Albert Museum in London. Laver wrote the Foreword for *Gerald Gardner – Witch!*, a biography by Jack Bracelin, from which the following is extracted:

> . . . It is true that he talked of strange things but he did so in a natural and humorous way that soon convinced me that I was in the presence of a man of a scientific and scholarly mind; a learned man, moreover, who had written the standard work on the Malayan kris, and was an anthropologist and archaeologist of distinction.
>
> But there was something else. It was impossible to meet Gerald Gardner without realizing that he was a great human being. He radiated friendliness and understanding. In spite of the screaming headlines of the sensational press he was quite plainly and obviously a *good* man.
>
> That first meeting is now many years ago, and I have seen no reason to change my opinion of his character, or my respect for his learning. Although I do not share all his opinions, he has taught me much. He has helped me in my own researches, and I am proud to think that I may have been of some little assistance to him in establishing his Museum of

Magic. That, and his books, are his lasting memorial, but it is his friendship that those who have been privileged to know him prize the most.

Reincarnation is a basic tenet of the Old Religion and, therefore, the Craft. Did Gerald Gardner speak about his thoughts on it when you were with him?

Yes, Gerald often mentioned the subject and, more especially, talked of his adventures in Cyprus and how he remembered one previous life in that country. He was always excited when he talked about his dreams and how he was shown what he did there. He even found what he was sure was the area where he had lived at that time, and bought the piece of land because of his convictions. He never seemed to tire of discussing it.

Of course, reincarnation was once a universal belief and is still held to be a perfectly natural occurrence in various parts of the world – particularly in India and certain cultures in the Far East. It has been spoken of by poets down the ages, and is present in Inner Rites of the Craft.

I found a beautiful reference to reincarnation in a personal hand-written book of Gerald's which was passed to me after his death, and this is what it says:

There be many Spiritual Powers not recognized as such – Music, Poetry, and the various forms of inspiration, and the greatest of all is Love. This is the first and last expression of Spirit. It may come naturally and the natural forms of spiritual power are ever better, but you are taught how power may be induced; in the more physical form at first, perhaps, but later in the more spiritual. This is the form that lasts beyond the grave, if it be wisely directed – but here a word of warning is necessary. Love directed beyond the grave is but a burden to the Spirit, if the loved one be not there to greet one, and it only means distaste for the others one meets, and so loneliness and unhappiness ensue.

There be rites which create and strengthen the bond between the souls; this forms a strain on the Astral – a pull, a dragging together, so causing their rebirth at about the same period and birth in similar conditions, for it would be useless if one were a Queen of Spain and the other a hotten-tot; so they must be of similar race and type. Then, they must be born and drawn together – to meet – to know and remember, however dimly. Memory be a curious thing, but it has rules; it remembers what is different! One remembers not the many strangers one meets at a tea-party for these are common, but who will forget performing the rites of the Goddess with the beloved? For these are to say the least, highly unusual, so form an extremely useful way to cause the strain on the Astral and the pulling together . . .

Did you ever meet Gerald's magical partner, Mrs Woodford-Grimes?

No, I did not, but I so wish that I had known her. I have two photographs of her, kindly given to me by Philip Heselton, and they show her to have been a beautiful, vibrant lady. She was also very talented and I learned that she was born in Malton, Yorkshire, so we shared the same county of birth, as well as both being adherents of the Craft, and friends of Gerald Gardner.

Ray Bone told me that she often drove Gerald from London to Christchurch to see Dafo (the name that Mrs Woodford-Grimes was known by to her friends) and one evening, while talking to Ray on the telephone, I asked her if she had spoken to Dafo about the New Forest coven. Ray said 'Yes', and that Dafo had said that the New Forest coven was an *hereditary* coven, not a traditional one, and had been quite definite about it. I then asked Ray if Dafo had ever mentioned the rite that was worked by that coven against Hitler's invasion of England in 1940, and Ray replied that she *had* asked Dafo about it, and Dafo had said, 'Oh yes, I was there, and Gerald and Dorothy Fordham too, among others. And Dorothy arranged it all.' So we have that information (apart from Gerald's own testimony) from the horse's mouth, so to speak.

Dafo had always been known by that name, but recently I have learned, on good authority, that this name was bestowed upon her as a child. It was a nickname or pet name, and one which she evidently liked enough to be known by in adulthood. If Dafo had been her Craft name, as has always been assumed, I hardly think she would have used it in everyday life. This had always puzzled me until I was otherwise informed.

Regarding the New Forest coven and their work against Hitler's invasion of England, in *The Diary of Virginia Woolf*, Volume 5, I came across the following entry for 12 September 1940: 'A gale has risen. Weather broken. Armada weather. No sound of planes today, only wind . . .' Remembering that this coven worked their magic on three separate occasions from Lammas Eve 1940 I thought this casual remark about the state of the weather not long afterwards was worth including. Mrs Woolf's mention of 'Armada weather' was curious. An avid reader, she must have suddenly thought of that earlier planned invasion and of the storms at sea which wrecked the Spanish ships and scattered them to the four winds. Then too, witches had worked to obstruct an invasion of British shores. In 1940, many occultists were working magic focused upon different aspects of 'Operation Sea-Lion' and the best ways to thwart it, and they succeeded!

Some time ago, while looking through some old newspapers, I came across a photocopy of a page from the *Daily Mirror* newspaper dated Wednesday 10 April 1957. It was an article by the then famous journalist, Marjorie Proops, entitled, 'I got the low-down on this witch lark! And had a devil of a time . . .' She was reporting on a story about a clairvoyant, and also upon her visit to a psychic lunch, where the chief speaker was a Dr Gerald Gardner. In a paragraph entitled 'How he started', Proops writes that she lured him into a quiet corner and asked him some questions, one of which was how he started. 'He said that twenty years ago he met a girl witch named Dafo and that was it.' Proops commented, 'Dafo brought out the occult in Gerald.' Twenty years before 1957 would have been 1937, which was around the time that Gerald and his wife, Donna, left London and went to live in Christchurch, Hampshire. And according to Philip Heselton, it was also the time when Dafo moved from Southampton to Christchurch.

Gerald always spoke very highly of Dafo, and obviously had a very close bond with her. His love for his wife, Donna, was undeniable, and she always held his heart, but Dafo embraced a different part of his life, and one moreover which held exciting discoveries for him in his search for spiritual fulfilment. With her, he found that the Goddess, whom he had already met and written about, was also known and worshipped by Dafo and the members of the New Forest coven. It *does* appear that they were fated to meet each other and, although they knew it not at the time, they were also fated to bring the Great Goddess back into the consciousness of thousands of people, both in the United Kingdom and in other parts of the world. However, this also involved bringing the Priesthood into the public eye, which to my mind was unfortunate to say the least. It has been so meddled with in recent times as to have almost lost its truth and its ancient teachings. Thankfully, though, it still retains many of its mysteries.

My friend and tutor, Jean MacDonald, said that she did not want the old rites to be lost, but at the same time stressed that they be given only to those who would uphold them and keep them secret. Even Jean had burned her book, thinking that at her age and because of her illness and living with in-laws who were Catholics she was unlikely to find the right person, or even an interested person, to whom she could pass on the rites. She was, happily, wrong! At the eleventh hour, as one might say, Jean saw me on television and took the chance of writing to me. She was staying in Durham at the time, and saw the programme on which Arnold and I were appearing as guests – *The David Jacobs Show*, being transmitted from Newcastle-upon-Tyne. Had Jean been at home in Inverness she would not have seen it. I believe that the Goddess, or the Ancient Providence, must have had a hand in it. If, as I also believe, your life pattern is written in the stars – even before your birth – then miraculous things *will* happen in your life, in some way, and at some time, if they are *meant* to happen.

The Cycle of the Moon (from 1945 to 1981) revealed (among other things) that the feminine principle in the form of the Goddess would again become known to the world. It was the *time* for this to occur. And even though Dafo was so frightened about the Craft being brought into the public eye and some form of persecution being brought down upon the heads of witches, not to mention the laws against it at that time, she was not to know the future, or the bigger picture that was to emerge from her friendship with Gerald Gardner.

Dafo was blessed with the psychic ability of clairvoyance. Gerald often commented upon different problems he had and used to say, 'I must ask Dafo about it'. What he meant was for Dafo to find the answer by using her sixth sense. An occasion arose when Arnold had a problem, and Gerald said he would contact Dafo and ask her to look into it for him. In her answer, Dafo said she had seen an object, but did not know how it connected with Arnold's problem. It was, in fact, the answer!

In your autobiography, Patricia, you mention visiting Donna Gardner's grave. Where exactly is it, and was she an initiate of the Craft?

Donna died in January 1960, and her body is buried in Ballabeg cemetery on the Isle of Man. Her gravestone carries a carved pentagram within a circle, and beneath the inscription to Donna is one to Gerald. Although Gerald's remains were buried at Tunis in North Africa, his friends thought it only right and proper to include his name on Donna's memorial stone.

When I last visited the grave, I left some everlasting flowers on it, and while I am sure that the local witches care for the grave, I hope that witches who visit the island will do the same. Ballabeg is only a few miles from Castletown and can be reached from Castletown via Arbory Road.

Gerald missed Donna dreadfully, and friends visited him and

stayed to look after him, as he was unable at that time to look after himself. And, although Gerald had invited Arnold and me over some time previously, owing to our engagements we didn't arrive there until the end of May 1960. Arnold had known Donna since 1939, when he first met Gerald at a lecture on folklore in London, and he was often invited to their home.

As to whether Donna was an initiate of the Craft, Gerald told me that she was not interested in it but did not mind him being involved. Apropos this question, a few years ago I was forwarded some papers from an initiate of one Charles Clark from Ayr, who had passed away. Clark had been an acquaintance of Gerald's and an initiate of the Craft and had had his own coven. I remember Gerald speaking about him and saying that Charles handled some of the many letters he received enquiring about the Craft, if they came from Charles's part of Scotland. Included with the papers I received was a photograph of a lady who was sky-clad (naked). She held a sword, which has since been recognized as one which had belonged to Gerald. It is an unusual sword, and can be seen in a photograph which appeared in the book, *Gerald Gardner – Witch!* This picture is of his wife, Donna, and behind her there is a collection of swords hung on the wall. One of these swords is identical to that in the photograph of the sky-clad lady. The caption to the photograph in the book reads, 'Donna, in the study of the Johore bungalow: behind her part of the collection'.

The sword in question is very different from a usual one, in that the blade is made in the manner of a Malayan kris (knife), with undulating curves from hilt to tip. It is, moreover, a very long sword and looks heavy. In the picture of the sky-clad lady, it is resting on the ground while she holds it with both hands, and it reaches nearly to her shoulder. I suppose it was only natural to assume (because she is sky-clad and holding a sword, however large and inappropriate) that the lady was a witch. She is wearing silver sandals, but no necklace. Recently, I have been assured that this lady was Donna Gardner. It certainly looks like Donna from other pictures I have seen of her, and the curtains and furniture in the photograph are of an Eastern influence. In fact, I would say that the photograph was taken in a room of Gerald's bungalow in Johore. I know that Gerald liked ladies to wear pretty sandals; he bought me a beautiful pair for a birthday present – gold, with sparkling ruby-coloured stones. This being so, it is not unlikely that he asked Donna to wear her sandals for the picture. But this picture is no proof of her being a witch by any stretch of the imagination. Gerald and Donna left Malaya on his retirement in January 1936, but back home in England his meeting with the witches and subsequent initiation into the Craft did not occur until *two or three years later*. So the photograph of the sky-clad Donna, taken in Johore, is merely a pretty picture of Gerald's wife, taken in the privacy of their home.

How then did Charles Clark come into possession of a photograph taken around fifty years previously? The person who sent me the papers said that he had received the negative of the photograph from Charles and had had it developed himself. In earlier times, it was not normal practice for High Street shops to process negatives of naked people, so Gerald must have found the negative buried somewhere and given it to Charles in the hope that he knew someone who would develop it for him, but evidently, it was forgotten.

Patricia, do you know what happened to the Witches' Mill after Gerald's death?

What indeed! I'm afraid the very thing that Gerald most feared and what he hoped would never occur did in fact take place. The entire contents of the museum were sold *nine* years after his passing. I have spoken elsewhere about the constant occurrence of 'nine' in terms of fateful years for Gerald, and here it was again, even though his physical life had ended.

The owner of the museum, Mrs Monique Wilson, apparently had a problem with alcohol, which was a great pity; and this along with other troubles, and a general disregard for her inheritance, was not good for the future of the museum.

A Mr William Worrall and his wife were engaged by Gerald to look after the museum, the ballroom and the restaurant, where they provided all the cooked meals on a daily basis. And in his will Gerald bequeathed the use of the museum and its attendant buildings to Mr Worrall with authority to continue his work and live in the cottage which was part of the Mill's buildings for as long as he wished. But sometime after Gerald's passing I received a very agitated letter from William. In it he complained that the Wilsons were making the lives of him and his wife intolerable. The Wilsons were interfering with the Worralls' work and often sat in the restaurant for hours staring at them in a hostile manner. They also went upstairs into the museum and unlocked all the cases of exhibits, encouraging the visitors to handle them. Had any items gone missing, William would have had to replace them. There were other instances of direct unpleasantness, so much so that William said he wanted out, and would Arnold and I be interested in buying his part in Gerald's will? Obviously, the Wilsons wanted him off the premises and were prepared to go to any lengths to obtain their ends. I'm afraid that we were not interested in the offer, and had no wish to become embroiled in these unsavoury matters. But I must say that we found both William and his wife to be decent and friendly people.

Around this time, there was the curious case of the missing items from the museum collection, which was shown on television one evening. These items had apparently been stolen, and the Wilsons were shown searching for them in the surrounding countryside. Some weeks later, another news item was broadcast on television which showed the artefacts being discovered by a visitor to the island. They were carefully wrapped, and hidden behind some rocks. All's well that ends. . . !

Many years later, my partner, Ian Lilleyman, and I took a holiday on the Isle of Man, and I renewed my acquaintance with Mr and Mrs Worrall. William told us that after much argument, the Wilsons had bought him out and taken over the cooking for the restaurant themselves. They soon tired of this occupation, however, and visitors became fewer. I thought how stupid that was when you had a couple like the Worralls with their excellent cooking to run the restaurant and look after the museum.

The reason why the business at the Witches' Mill became run down was nothing more than bad management. It only struggled because the Wilsons became disinterested in it. Neither is it true to state that the story in the *News of the World* newspaper about their daughter, Yvette, being initiated into the Craft at the age of four had anything at all to do with the Wilsons deciding to move to Spain and buy a bar in Torremolinos. They spoke to the newspaper willingly and even had pictures taken showing their witchcraft ceremonies. And, instead of ignoring Gerald's wishes, they could have sold the museum, both contents and premises, as a going concern, without destroying it by selling its contents to Ripley's, in the USA.

The witch, Angus MacLeod, who lived in Castletown and had known Gerald, was around when the men from Ripley's arrived to pack up the exhibits. Angus said there was a huge pile of papers and letters in the centre of the ballroom floor, and the Wilsons told him that he could have all of them and do what he liked with them. So, after saving some books (in Gerald's handwriting) and other interesting items, Angus made a bonfire on his part of the beach and burned the lot.

Over the years, the Mill and its attendant buildings have been sold and resold several times, and my witch friends on the island have told me that it has now been sold again, and the buildings turned into cottages and flats. The Mill itself has been converted into living accommodation with three bedrooms and a Victorian spiral staircase. I wonder if the old Arbory witches would have approved? Gerald had reported in his museum guide that the old windmill, known as the 'Witches' Mill', had been there since at least 1611, as it was mentioned in a court record of that date. The guide continues:

The Mill got its name because the famous Arbory witches lived close by there, and the story goes that when the old mill was burned out in 1848 they used the ruins as a dancing-ground, for which, as visitors may see, it was eminently suited, being round inside to accommodate the witches' circle, while the remains of the stone walls screened them from the wind and from prying eyes.

After being abandoned for many years, the large barns of the Mill were taken in 1950 to house the only Museum in the world devoted to Magic and Witchcraft. . . . The only recorded execution of a witch in the Isle of Man took place within a short distance of the old Mill, when in 1617 Margaret Ine Quane and her young son were burned alive at the stake near the Market Cross in Castletown. She had been caught trying to work a fertility rite to get good crops; and, as this was in the time when the Lordship of Man was temporarily in the hands of the witch-hunting King James I, she suffered the extreme penalty. A memorial to Margaret Ine Quane, and to the victims of the witch persecutions in Western Europe, whose total numbers have been estimated at nine million, is in the Museum.

The Arbory witches were well known and it is possible that their ancestors had known Margaret Ine Quane. She may even have belonged to one of their covens. There were witches in the Isle of Man hundreds of years before the museum came into existence. I cited evidence of them in my autobiography, *One Witch's World* (paperback title *High Priestess*).

It was a very good thing that Gerald Gardner bought the mill and the museum from Cecil Williamson when he did. Gerald introduced the public to a more factual view of witchcraft than that of Williamson, who mainly concentrated upon the sensational aspects of black magic, coupled almost entirely with the imagery of witches as Devil-worshipping crones. These two men were poles apart in their ideas and intentions. Williamson was chiefly concerned with drawing the crowds through the then popular image of witches (which can be likened to articles in the 'gutter' press) whereas Gerald Gardner's heart and mind were concentrated upon what he knew, as an initiate of the Craft, and in bringing a more truthful picture of witchcraft to the general public. I believe that Gerald was definitely inspired by the Goddess in this, irrespective of any monetary gain, although he was astute enough to realize that any business venture must be viewed in that light as well.

Incidentally, when the museum was first opened on 29 July 1951 it was called 'The Folklore Centre of Superstition and Witchraft'. The opening ceremony was performed by Gerald, who was then described as 'the resident witch'. At the same time, I was working in a summer season show at the Town Hall, Holyhead, Anglesey. We were both on islands, and a straight line can be drawn on a map from Castletown down to Holyhead, over the Irish Sea. But it was to be a further nine years (!) before Gerald and I met, in 1960.

Did Gerald ever say that witches could alter the Book of Shadows to suit the High Priestess's tastes?

Gerald would never have made such an idiotic and irresponsible statement. The basic ways of working should not be changed, principally because they have been tried and tested over the years, and proved to be effective. The rituals have a long lineage and, had they been found wanting, they would have been altered long before the present day.

If a High Priestess wishes to add poetry or pieces of prose, or even new rituals, which are appropriate to the proceedings, well and good, but any addition to the Book of Shadows should be accompanied by the author's name and the date it was entered. If a High Priestess dislikes the ways of working, she should stand down.

This question reminds me of an initiate in one coven who, after a period of at least two years, informed the leaders that she was averse to any purification. This statement, however, came after the lady had been informed that she was not yet ready to be advanced to the position of High Priestess. A case of sour grapes? *Gerald Gardner was said to be very proud of his Scottish ancestry, but recently it has been called into question. Although the subject is trivial when put against his work in restoring the Old Religion, Patricia, I would be interested to hear your comments.*

Like you, I find this another unnecessary attack upon Gerald's character by people who never knew him. There *is* evidence of his roots, however, so the doubters have not looked far. In *Gerald Gardner – Witch!*, the author states that Gerald was proud of his Scottish roots, and that:

> ... the family had never forgotten that it was of Scottish ancestry, and they traced their descent still further, to Simon le Gardinor, born in the fourteenth century. Through three centuries they had remembered the highland country of their grandsires ...

Gerald's detractors seem to have overlooked his Last Will and Testament, too. In it he left his grandfather's dirk (Scottish dagger), his grandfather's skean dhu (black-handled knife) and his grandfather's sword with its cross belt (known as the 'Rhyming Sword'), together with two other Scottish items he had acquired himself, to his sister-in-law Miriam Gardner. In the event of her predeceasing him they were left to Miriam Gardner's son and daughter. Gerald expresses the wish that the articles be treated as heirlooms and remain in the Gardner family. That does not sound to me as though Gerald merely dreamed up a Scottish ancestry; they are the words of a man who is anxious for these items to be left in the family as a reminder of their Scottish origins.

We must not forget that some of Gerald's ancestors achieved distinguished positions in their careers. Alan Gardner joined the Royal Navy in 1755 when he was only thirteen and commanded his own ship before the age of twenty-five. He later became a Vice-Admiral, a member of parliament, and then a peer, Baron Gardner of Uttoxeter. In 1807 he fought against Napoleon's invasion of Britain as commander-in-chief of the Channel Fleet. Other ancestors became mayors of Liverpool.

Where is Gerald Gardner buried? I have heard that it is in Tunis but do not know exactly where. Do you know, Patricia?

Gerald's body was originally buried on 13 February 1964 in the Belvedere Cemetery, Carthage, Tunisia and, although I thought his body should have been brought home and buried in Donna's grave in the Isle of Man, Mr and Mrs Wilson (to whom Gerald left the bulk of his estate) said that he should stay where he had died. However, in some ways it was appropriate that he was buried at Carthage as the city was once an important centre for the worship of the Great Goddess.

In 1968, the late High Priestess, Eleanor Bone, learned from the Tunisian authorities that the Belvedere Cemetery was to be turned into a park. She was told that, if she wished, the remains of her friend could be re-interred in another cemetery, so she travelled to Tunis to make the arrangements. A number of us, with the exception of the Wilsons, contributed to Eleanor's expenses, and Gerald's remains were moved on 24 October 1968 to the Christian Cemetery (formerly known as the Cimetière de Borgel) Keiredine Pacha Street, Tunis. The grave is situated in Section F, Carre 4, Plot 246.

Some months ago I received a visit from Larry Jones, a High Priest of the Craft who lives in Canada. His profession often takes him to the Middle East and I asked him whether it would be possible for him to visit Gerald's grave in Tunis. Larry said it certainly would be possible so, armed with the details and whereabouts of the cemetery, this likeable person whom I consider to be someone who means what he says, departed for Canada, with assurances of informing me when he was able to visit Tunis.

After several weeks, Larry rang to say that he had found Gerald's grave, which was an unmarked, overgrown, rubble-strewn plot, and sent pictures to illustrate his findings. Photocopies of the interment records were denied, as were photographs of the records. The next day, Larry made arrange-ments with a local mason to provide a low, flat, stone marker for the grave and for the ground to be levelled and cleaned up. And, before leaving, he also applied for permits for the work to be carried out. He said that nothing is done quickly in that part of the world, but continued to keep in touch with the mason.

One day, he rang to say that Gerald's birth and death dates had been engraved upon the stone. I thought that Gerald deserved some words to describe his major achievements in life. Was this possible? Larry said it was, depending upon the various difficulties already experienced. Happily, they were overcome! The inscription I chose is as follows:

Gerald Brosseau Gardner
13th June 1884 – 12th February 1964
Author – Archaeologist – Artist
Father of modern Wica and beloved of the Great Goddess

Larry Jones is to be congratulated for performing this act of remembrance for Gerald Gardner, long overdue for someone who at the very least deserves a marked grave. And, for this High Priest of the Craft to appear who, in the course of his work, actually travels to the Middle East and was willing to undertake the commission, is to me yet another example of the Ancient Providence granting the highly improbable!

What brought about your decision to move away from Gerald's coven?

This is the first time I have heard that I had belonged to Gerald's coven! Arnold and I visited him many times on the Isle of Man, and he came over to be present at our meetings on numerous occasions. Once, he travelled from Castletown to our home and officiated at our Handfasting the night before Arnold and I were married in a civil ceremony at the Sheffield Register Office. Gerald was, of course, guest of honour at our celebratory luncheon at the Grand Hotel in the city.

Gerald had a small coven in Castletown, and sometimes when we were visiting him we worked with them, but it would have been impossible to belong to that coven, all those miles away. When I had earned my spurs and had achieved the title of High Priestess, I was at liberty to form my own coven, a somewhat time-consuming process as you may realize. Today, the Sheffield Coven has been in operation for forty-seven years and, during that time, many witches after gaining the Third Degree have hived off to form their own covens. Quite a few of my early members have passed to the Summerland, too.

Gerald also had a coven at Bricket Wood near St Albans, and he invited us down there one Samhain, when we attended the meeting in the Witch's Cottage (which Gerald owned) in the woods of Five-Acres Sun Club. (The full story of that visit can be found in my autobiography.)

Is there any proof that Gerald actually earned a doctorate?

The documentation for Gerald's doctorate in philosophy, along with a certificate, is held by the New Wiccan Church International of Canada in Toronto. The entry, in Gerald Gardner's Library, reads as follows:

> Diploma from the Meta Collegiate Extension of the National Electronic Institute graduating G.B. Gardner with the degree of Doctor of Philosophy signed Sept 21, 1937 by Ernest Stevens, J.F. Lyons, E.G. Hill and G. Pappas.

The degree was given by publication, no doubt for his academic work *Kris and other Malay Weapons* published in 1936 and subsequently used by museums in all parts of the world.

8 Initiation and Ritual

Despite the many disclosures about the Craft over the years, which naturally involved the breaking of the oath taken at initiation, the Mysteries still hold a potency and a power which remain untarnished.

I well remember my own initiation into the Craft of the Wise. It was difficult for me to realize that this strange and new experience was happening to me. My mind was suddenly confronted with something out of the ordinary – something which seemed to be very ancient yet very real and almost totally of the spirit. And beyond these impressions was a sense of the entire proceedings echoing the natural processes of human life. The stages of the Degrees, which followed in the course of time, were equally awe-inspiring and nothing has ever dimmed what Gerald called that 'initial sense of wonder'.

Apart from initiations, which have a different purpose, rituals are designed to elevate the consciousness to more spiritual levels so that the participants are able to contact higher vibrations. Ritual also enhances and energizes the vital-force centres (or chakras) in the body, and so aids in developing and harmonizing these subtle forces within ordinary living levels. Performed well, ritual is by far the best method for attuning the mind and contacting the World of Spirit.

Certain covens in the States start a meeting by dancing before *the Circle is cast. Is this how you were taught?*

I have never heard of dancing *before* a Circle is cast and, unless this is done at a festival when things are more free and easy, I cannot see what benefit there is in this. Gerald taught me to *conserve* my energy and sit quietly for a while prior to a ritual or a meeting. The whole idea is to start refreshed and filled with energy and life-force. We have a period of meditation in which we zero down to nil – or no thing – before the Circle is cast. Only then is the Circle truly cast, and in this way you are creating a miniature cosmos if you like, from nothing – or no-thing. And you continue to build it. First, near the ground, as you draw the Circle; then a little higher, as you consecrate it with water; next, perfuming it with incense, when you carry the burner, higher still, round the Circle; and finally invoking the Mighty Ones, at the top-most point. These actions, of course, equate with the Four Elements. First the Earth, drawing the Circle near the ground; then the consecration with Water; the smoke from the incense floating in the Air; and the invocation of the Mighty Ones, which is easily identified with Fire – the purest element.

The Dance itself is the first and last expression of a Magic Circle, and is one of the best ways of raising the Cone of Power; so, wasting your energies by dancing prior to a meeting, when they may be required for some important magical work, is not the most sensible thing to do. In the old days, it was the custom to hold a feast and a dance *after* an esbat or a sabbat, but these activities were suspended when the persecutions began.

Of his initiation, which took place in one of Dorothy Fordham's beautiful homes – the Mill House, at the top of Chewton Glen in Highcliffe – Gerald Gardner wrote:

I found that Old Dorothy and some like her, plus a number of New Forest people, had kept the light shining. It was, I think, the most wonderful night of my life. In true witch fashion we had a dance afterwards, and kept it up until dawn.

Are the Mighty Ones (invoked at the Four Gates of the Circle) conceived as being called up from the Underworld, and are they the same as the Blessed Dead?

The Mighty Ones are the Kings of the Elements so, no, they are not 'called up' from the Underworld. They are known by different names in different traditions of magic and these are usually in Latin, so are very difficult to pronounce. In any case, these names do not belong to the West and are alien to witchcraft, as we know it. Some witches use the Qabalistic names for the Mighty Ones; they are easier to pronounce and do have links with the Western Mystery Tradition. They are as follows: Raphael – Air; Michael – Fire; Gabriel – Water; and Auriel – Earth. These beings are known to Qabalists as the Four Great Archangels. They exist and operate in their own particular spheres of life and can be called upon for aid in magical workings, providing the work is within their specialist functions. They are also sexless, being constructed from pure consciousness, and can be brought into our mental pictures as we think they would look, or from traditional images of them.

Most witches usually invoke these great Intelligences by calling them the 'Mighty Ones', at the same time conjuring up a suitable elemental scene at the appropriate Gates of the Circle. My Scottish informant, Jean MacDonald, when describing a particular rite to me, wrote: 'You go to the Four Winds . . .' In the ancient Gaelic tradition, this is how they knew the four points of the compass, and Jean's long tradition in the north of Scotland would undoubtedly have had strong links with the Gaelic Celts. They were called the 'Four Airts' and had attributes based upon the quality of the prevailing winds in Britain. The East Wind is cold and dry; the South Wind is warm and dry; the West Wind is warm and wet; and the North Wind is cold and wet.

Regarding the second part of the question: the Mighty Ones have no connection with the Blessed Dead and should not be confused with them.

Are there Mysteries which are given only from one High Priestess to another High Priestess, and between High Priests?

Yes.

Why do initiations involve the emotions of joy and terror?

They heighten the senses and make aspirants aware of greater forces than themselves. Unless an initiation arouses these feelings within an aspirant, one might as well forget all about it. The ancient form of initiation into the Craft held greater trials and tests than the initiations of today, which are more or less watered-down versions of the original. These tests were performed for the initiates' benefit, and to awaken them to the seriousness of initiation and what it stands for. In this respect, if an aspirant failed these trials (which were within a normal person's power to accomplish), they would be sent on their way until they had 'grown' and had cultivated more courage and confidence in themselves. The Mysteries of the Goddess are a Path for the evolution of the soul and not to be undertaken lightly. All spiritual Paths carry similar messages. However, as I have said before, the Goddess will lead you as a mother leads her child, and this tenet is based upon Love and Trust – 'Perfect Love for the Goddess and Perfect Trust in the Goddess' – a dictum which sadly has been misinterpreted in recent times.

A life usually contains many episodes of happiness and sorrow, success and failure – highs and lows – and the Craft teaches you that a philosophical attitude must be nurtured, and that through following and practising the ways of the Craft this will be all the easier to accomplish. Happiness and sorrow should be regarded as purification for the soul. Both emotions are necessary on the Path.

A person who wishes to evolve through the Mysteries must have attained a certain level of knowledge to begin with, and this is best perceived by the leaders of a coven. No good could ever come from initiating someone who wants to run before they can walk. Of course, it must be realized that the Higher Self will always be aware that human experience is but a learning process, but by practising the rites, which are intended to elevate the consciousness, much of the dross of the Lower Self will be drained away leaving a clarity of mind, a pathway more attuned to the Higher Self.

Many initiates in the Craft find that things do not always go their way after their initiation. This, I was told by both Gerald and Jean, was the Goddess's way of assessing your strength and determination to succeed in your quest. Jean said:

> The Goddess watches you and waits to see if you are worthy and have the necessary qualities to succeed and overcome difficulties. And, when She is satisfied with you, you will find that things start to move in the right direction and you get on the up and up.

And I have found this to be so.

When you are initiated, you are born again through the Triangle of the Goddess, and thus become a Child of the Goddess. Henceforth, your 'Mother' will love you and teach you. You have but to *listen* and to *trust* in Her.

Why use the old calendar dates for the cross-quarter festivals?

Pope Gregory XIII reformed the Julian calendar in 1582 and in the process twelve days were lost from the calendar year. Also, an extra day (29th February) was added every four years (leap year). But it was still based on the Julian or Old Style solar calendar. The latter was introduced by Julius Caesar in the first century BC, and was developed from an earlier Moon-based calendar.

The new dates are therefore not in harmony with the nature year: they are twelve days *behind* the old dates and before the peak of each of the Four Tides is reached. This occurs at 15° of the four fixed signs of the Zodiac.

The advantages of working magic with knowledge of the Four Tides cannot be too strongly emphasized. This, then, is why many witches prefer to use the old calendar dates for magical projects and for celebrating the cross-quarter festivals.

Is the passing of the power the true initiation of the Second Degree?

I would say that it is one of the most important parts of the Second Degree, or Initiation Proper. Another is the blessing, but these things cannot be divorced from the ritual which encompasses the whys and the wherefores of this Degree. In other words, the entire structure of the ritual grants the necessary steps which illuminate and inform the Initiate as to the seriousness and benefit of this undertaking.

Regarding initiation, Pat: how long do you feel a person should wait prior to acceptance or rejection?

The popular period of a year and a day is just not sufficient in most cases. There is no hard and fast rule about this, but there must come a point when a decision is reached; I have found it to be within eighteen moons.

In the Degree system, what are your criteria for elevating members to the Second and Third Degrees?

The Degrees of elevation show again that a learning process is involved. There is also an Inner awakening – a spiritual and mystical awakening – which I am sure that most witches understand. These Degrees have always been an integral part of the Priesthood of the Old Religion, and for the same reasons that other religions (perhaps not so magical) train those souls who wish to serve their deities in this manner. Therefore, in the way that I was taught, for a member of my coven to attain the Second Degree – the Initiation Proper – they must: have a thorough knowledge of the magical implements; know the Four Tides;

show competence in ways of working magic; and have success-fully performed at least three magical workings on their own. These are some of the requirements because, when they progress through that Degree, they are required to demonstrate their abilities in this way. Further, they will take a magical name which should harmonize with their future progress, and by which they will be known in the Circle, until such time as they feel the need for a different one.

The Third Degree is not so much a Degree as a magical rite. It should only be bestowed if a witch of the Second Degree wishes to form a new coven, or practise with a partner, in his or her own temple. It may also be given if a witch, who is functioning in the Second Degree, is moving away from the area, but hopes to form a new coven in the future.

The whole thing about the Magic Circle is that, as a miniature cosmos, it moves, grows and turns, and sometimes changes what is within it, and even what is extraneous to it.

There seems to be a lot of 'ego-tripping' when witches meet at social gatherings and moots. The Degrees are spoken of as though there is no knowledge of their sacred and secret meanings, but merely as a way of impressing listeners. These so-called witches apparently air their positions in the Craft to all and sundry as though they were speaking of a win on the lottery, or some such trivial game. All this leaves a very large question mark as to their origins and does the Craft no favours at all.

I have heard that some of the old covens, despite being uncertain of a newcomer, would nevertheless proceed with their initiation. Why was this?

There was definitely a method in their madness. They had found that soon after the initiation the true motives of the individual would be revealed to them, often within the following three weeks – whether good or ill. That is why the old covens (and some of the later ones) would go ahead with the initiation, even if there was the smallest doubt. And what if the worst was discovered? Well, the First Degree is not the initiation proper and action could be taken related to the nature of the person's unsuitability to be an initiate. Other covens would be warned about them and sometimes a rite would be performed to prevent them from troubling the Craft again. It all depended upon what their motives were. A person can realize their mistakes and become worthy initiates in the future.

The Goddess has to be satisfied about an initiate first. I know that She has prevented a coven meeting from taking place. And it is only later, through hindsight, that it is realized why this apparently annoying reversal of plans was the best thing that could have occurred. The Goddess is also known to impede a witch from being present at a meeting. At the last minute, something will happen to hinder a witch from attending. And this can be for any number of reasons, and not negative ones either. But, sure enough, the purpose will become all too clear after the event.

What do you think is important for leaders to teach new people coming into the Craft?

The things you were taught upon your own initiation. All the basic essentials concerning the Circle – the structure of it; the weapons; the festivals; and understanding why the rituals are performed sky-clad. (It is important for new people to understand why the initiations cannot be performed wearing clothes. You are 'born' into the Craft, and you ain't born wearing clothes!) Aspirants should learn the basics so thoroughly that they become second nature and they don't have to stop and think about them first, or say, 'Oh yes, I know this, now what is it? I knew all about this before I came . . .' etc., etc. That will not do!

Once initiated, they should practise and experiment as much as possible. Practice makes perfect, so they should practise the Art, using some of the Eight Ways to the Centre, and keep to a regular schedule if possible, twice a week or once a week. And it is no good attempting anything if tired or worried. If such is the case, they should leave it for another day. But if a person is worried about something, they should commune with the Goddess or the God, and ask for help and guidance in the matter. This is the first thing to do, and They will always provide the answer in one way or another.

Practising the Craft is much better for growth than reading about it all the time. There are psychic and other magical abilities which can develop through this dedication – clairvoyance, clairaudience and other forms of heightened perception. Scrying is a very worthwhile exercise to perform on your own in the Circle. Little and often is the rule here, and do not be discouraged if nothing happens immediately.

Each witch will usually have their own particular esoteric subject they want to learn, such as astrology, runes, tarot etc; and this is where books come into the picture. When proficiency is acquired and the subject thoroughly mastered, any psychic gifts a witch may have will automatically come into play to enhance their learning. The very act of studying such subjects will aid any latent psychic ability to develop and manifest, and sometimes this occurs quite suddenly and without warning.

It is also important for 'young' witches to make pilgrimages to sacred sites through which they can make contact with the ancient gods. The physical effort which is often required to reach a site is as necessary to their spiritual development as time spent in meditation or prayer before an altar. It is also quite common-place for people to receive something of value at these ancient monuments, such as a poetic verse, a melody or a special 'message'. An idea for a painting may flash into the mind, to be translated later into a beautiful picture. It is advisable however, if you visit a site with other people, to spend some of the time, quietly, on your own.

A new witch must also be enlightened as to the *nature* of the Goddess and Her Consort, and how They, if requested through adoration and prayer, will always answer a petition – but in the way They choose, and according to the sense of a petition. New witches must also learn to keep their mouths shut and not blab to all and sundry about Craft matters, or indeed anything of a magical nature, as this would ensure that their progress in these things would not be forthcoming.

There are some people who regard the Mysteries as an interesting exercise – something which satisfies their thirst for contact with the Old Gods and for the unusual; but they lack the ability to recognize them as a means of spiritual progress. Some souls are quite happy to attend meetings but fail to understand that, unless they work by themselves between times, they will never attain *that* which the Craft embodies and which is represented by the Crowned Pentagram. Above all, they must realize that initiation into the Craft of the Wise is an extremely serious matter – that they are embarking upon a journey as important as their birth into this world and that, unless they are willing to endure any negative karma (which initiation usually invokes), the Craft is not yet for them. Nothing less than a sense of awe, a childlike trust, and an honourable and open nature is acceptable.

New initiates must also realize that the Craft is one of the oldest living traditions of a priesthood in the world. That, despite what they have read or heard by detractors of the Craft (whose efforts are mainly focused upon getting rid of a matriarchal religion), it was practised from ancient times; continued in secret during the persecutions of the witches; and today has emerged again as Wicca, the fastest-growing religion in the Western World. That this is so, we have to thank Gerald Brosseau Gardner who returned to Britain in the late autumn of his years, and wrought the magical renaissance of the Old Religion.

Many people today scoff at the idea of initiation and start for themselves. How do you view this development? Are so-called self-initiated witches 'valid'?

If people scoff at the Craft's methods of initiation into the Mysteries, it reveals their ignorance, and that their knowledge of the Mysteries is negligible. It reminds me of the saying, 'It is better to keep your mouth shut and be thought a fool, than to open it and remove all doubt.' As I see it, 'Wicca' represents everyone who worships the

Goddess and Her Consort, in whatever ways they prefer. The Priesthood, on the other hand, is exactly that. It has always existed to perform the magical practices of the Craft, and to initiate those who are suitable to be trained for the Priesthood in the future. It also contains those witches to whom the evolution of the soul is all-important, and who are dedicated enough to take the serious step of initiation.

I cannot see how self-initiated witches can be 'valid', as you put it. Certainly not in the sense of having been initiated into the Craft by an ordained priest or priestess, whereby the blessing is given and, later, Passing of the Power. It is said that the quintessence of initiation, *lies with the one who gives it*, when these numinous gifts are bestowed.

The advent of DIY witches is a development which reveals that these people are doing something about their spiritual growth, and so long as they are *au fait* with the Craft tenet, 'If it harms none, do what ye will', which by the way does not mean you can do any old thing, but *follow and perform your true will*. If that is understood, I see no reason why they should not 'do their own thing', as it were.

Is there an advantage in making your own ritual tools versus those ready-made from a shop?

Fashioning your own tools confers a very great advantage, as you put your own energy and individuality, and also your personality, into the making of them, so that they are truly a part of you. But, unfortunately, not everyone is able to make athames or swords: they need a professional hand. Pentacles are possible if you buy a suitable round or square piece of copper or brass. Gerald made mine from an odd piece of brass taken from a defunct inscription off a coffin lid, which he had obtained trawling round workshops in Douglas (Isle of Man). Many witches make their own wands from a branch of a hazel tree, cut on a Wednesday – the day given to Mercury (or Hermes), the god of knowledge, inspiration, and even divination, who is known as 'The Messenger'.

In the old days, bone or ivory were used for some tools, because they once had life in them. Witches however, are never at a loss in finding solutions to problems. During the persecution times, their tools had to seem like ordinary kitchen utensils, and be mixed with them, in case a witchfinder called. If they possessed a sword, this would have to be carefully wrapped and buried somewhere, until the danger had passed. Any markings on tools would be erased, too. If a witch had a very secure place in which to hide their tools, they may have used that, but it was still risky. Who would have thought that one day ritual artefacts would actually be available from a shop? Certainly not our predecessors!

For a robed ritual, are there any stipulations relating to the garments?

Robes should be comfortable to wear and made in a colour which the wearer likes. Some occultists favour white or black. White, although not strictly a colour, reflects light, given out or taken in, while black absorbs anything negative within itself. It all depends upon the system of magic being worked. Some groups decide upon a colour and everyone has a robe of whatever colour is chosen, which certainly brings cohesion and equilibrium to those taking part, while others prefer a robe in a colour of their own choosing which suits them and harmonizes with their personalities.

Robes should not have wide sleeves as these are liable to catch on items like candlesticks and knock them over. They should always have hoods attached to them, as a hood is excellent for a meditative interval or for withdrawing into oneself for the purpose of concentration. A hood also keeps the head warm if working a ritual outdoors and the weather is cold. But hoods need only be worn when the necessity arises.

Most robes are of the straight cassock-style, with a special girdle to hold them in place. This girdle should be fastened firmly, as it is symbolic of a private, immediate circle which protects our intentions and our true wills. It is usually knotted with a reef knot which does not slip. The girdle should be in a colour which harmonizes with the shade of robe but stands out from the robe so that it can be clearly seen.

If working indoors, the feet should be bare and free to move in the pattern of the rite, and underclothes kept to a minimum, although most ritualists prefer to be naked beneath the robe.

For those not cognizant with the meaning of wearing robes, I will explain further. Robing-up, as it is called, represents casting off the everyday self in preparation for work of the spirit. It should never be done carelessly, as though you were dressing up for a party or some other frivolous occasion. When you don your robe, your mind should be intent upon the ceremony at hand and, in adjusting the robe, you should be making the Inner adjustments of your spiritual self for the rite to come. The robe is nothing more nor less than a means of blocking out the mundane world and stepping into a higher state of consciousness. Because, unless there is this switching on or lighting up within, any external accessories will serve no purpose at all. A short mantra such as 'I am casting off my mundane self with these garments, and donning this apparel to blend with my higher self', should help this transformation to take place. When not being worn, robes and girdles should be kept apart from everyday clothing.

I have come across one or two examples of would-be occultists who were totally uninformed as to the wearing of robes. On one occasion, a lady appeared in a revealing voile dress, which was split at the side to show her thigh and had a plunging neckline which plunged too far. The leader of another group had instructed the members fully about robes, but one female entered the ritual site in a long sleeveless evening dress! It was very beautiful, but quite absurd for the occasion. If a person's vanity comes before their intelligence, occultism is not for them.

Mrs Crowther, does music improve the rituals and proceedings within the Circle?

Very much so! And not only in the Circle. Music has been a part of the Old Religion in many different cultures for a long time. It is an important way of attaining at-one-ment with the Divine. In Ancient Egypt for example, the Cat-Headed Goddess, Bast, delighted in dancing and music and even holds a sistrum in her statuary. Herodotus has given us a brief description of a festival of Bast. He says that at least 700, 000 people attended the festival. Most of them came by water, and as they sailed along women played castanets and the men flutes, while others sang and clapped to the music. The festival of Hathor at Dendera was an equally great occasion. Above the sound of hymns to Hathor were the notes of the lute and the rattle of the sistrum. Considering that temples to the Old Gods throughout the Middle East were huge buildings, often larger than the later Christian cathedrals, there must have been galleries of musicians and singers performing for the multitude. At the time of the New Empire it was also the custom for large numbers of women to enrol as singers and musicians in the temples of all the gods, especially those dedicated to Amoun Ra, the great horned god of the Ancient Egyptians.

During the witch persecutions, the trials proved that music was an integral part of the meetings. It was played by the leader or another member of the coven who was known as the 'Devil's Piper'. The tabor, pipe, trump (Jew's harp) or fiddle were popular in both Scotland and England. The Somerset witches spoke of the 'Man in Black' playing on a pipe or cittern while they danced.

Music affects the emotional or astral body and raises the consciousness to a higher level, often felt as a tingling and some-times a cold, shivery sensation on the flesh. Of course, there are many different kinds of music but, if it is played for religious or magical purposes, it is usually a melody that is known by the coven or group to evoke the transformation and give a feeling of exhilaration and happiness.

People have different preferences for music, and the type one person appreciates will do nothing for another. In a coven, a library of music is often built up which is approved by all the members. Suitable pieces for diverse rituals and occasions will then be at hand to enhance the proceedings. We are very lucky today, being able to purchase players with which the most brilliant orchestrations, simple folk tunes, or any kind of music can be employed within the Circle.

There should also be a variety of sonics and effects which equate with Seasonal Rites, the Elements, the Planets, Meditation, and every type of rite likely to be worked by a coven. The Drum is an excellent stimulant of the sexual centres in Circumambulation, the Dance, and in the building of the Cone of Power, for its incessant rhythm and compulsion. The Knock has an immediate effect as a call for attention, or enacted in a series of numbers which relate to a particular planet, or as a sacred number in a ritual. The Knock creates a slight shock and can be valuable at a certain point in a rite when a signal is needed. Another important instrument especially associated with the Craft is the Horn. This has a long history in witchcraft rites. One of its main uses today is for summoning the Lords of the Outer Spaces at the Four Gates of the Circle, and *before* each invocation is pronounced. Its effect upon listeners is of a connection between Outer and Inner Intelligences and it gives a feeling of expectation. Blown softly, the Horn can also be used at the end of a rite to signify a stepping-down of consciousness to ordinary, mundane levels. The sound reverberating in the ear aids a gradual transference from Inner to Outer contacts and activities. The witches of old blew the horn on the top of hills to invoke the Old Gods – the ancient powers of Life and Death. The urgency and 'other-worldly' effect it created in the darkness would also have lent itself to a shifting of the consciousness into a higher state of awareness.

Most modern witches insert a reed into the mouthpiece of a horn. Choosing a reed with a suitable note is essential for occult workings; a too-high note, or a too-low note, would not produce the required resonance, so try a few different reeds in the middle register of the scale, such as a lower F or an E, until you find the one that gives the most rich and melodiously satisfying sound. If easy to fit, you could have a few reeds of different notes and interchange them when the need arises.

The Bell is also an important adjunct to ritual matters and plays a significant part in initiations. It produces a sonic which reverberates gradually into silence, and advanced occultists and witches will follow the sonic, inwardly, from the physical to the spiritual levels and energies – from the audible to the inaudible – thereby harmonizing their astral bodies and spiritual selves upon Inner as well as Outer levels of Being. A bell has to be chosen very carefully. Brass bells are no use at all; they have no reverberations and no pure tones, or so I have found. One of the best is a Tibetan bell or Cow bell; they are made from bronze and they have the most beautiful tones. I am lucky to possess a Tibetan bell. It has a wooden clapper or beater which is almost the length of the bell itself and gives a pure resonating note.

The Voice, being directly a part of the operator's physicality and invoking responses from hearers both human and divine, is thus, the instrument *par excellence* for sonic communication as all other sonic devices, however helpful, are mechanical. Speech and vocalizations are invaluable aids in ritual. The timbre of the voice, if well trained, attended by its owner's passionate declamation, will automatically infect the participants with a similar enthusiasm and raise a rite to the required spiritual dimensions. A voice however needs practice and training, and a rite will fail if the voice is inept or incoherent or is lacking in other ways.

Again, I must elucidate that initiates become more competent in any number of ways, through allegiance to the Goddess and Her Consort.

The sounds of Nature should not be forgotten. They are excellent in seasonal rites, when an element is described, and for a period of meditation which harmonizes with an element. Water has a variety of sounds such as that of the sea, a waterfall, a running brook, or even raindrops spattering upon leaves. Fire can be recorded best from a boon-fire, while it is possible for Air to be captured when a strong wind or gale is blowing. Earth can be achieved by the sounds of digging it, or recording someone's footsteps tramping upon fallen autumn leaves.

This question about music reminded me of something concerning my partner, Ian Lilleyman. He had no interest in music as such until quite recently, when he suddenly announced that he wanted to learn to play a tin whistle! He bought several, together with a book entitled *Instant Tin Whistle*, and practised for at least two hours most nights. He has progressed to being able to play dozens of tunes proficiently. Ian then said that he would like to learn the flute! Being close to the twenty-fifth anniversary of our Handfasting, I bought him a silver flute, silver being the metal given on that anniversary. Lessons from a teacher of the instrument are taken every week and, although the flute is more difficult to learn than a whistle, Ian is doing well. He says that these instruments have taken him over, and I have often wondered if he was a musician in a previous life and planetary influences have occurred in his natal chart which have suddenly reawakened this interest. Or has the Goddess had a hand in it? Whatever the cause, it was a remarkable occurrence and I am very pleased that the Orphic Path has opened up for him in this way. It echoes the years of practice with which the house was filled when I first started learning to become a professional musician.

I am not involved in the Craft myself, but I have heard there are sexual rites practised by witches. Is this true?

I wondered when this type of question would come along! The rites of the Craft were initially drawn from the Old Religion, and sex in the Old Religion was regarded as sacred. Men and women were made in the likeness of the gods, and therefore the human form was also regarded in the same way.

Procreation was seen in a similar light and as the means by which a soul incarnated – another human being came into existence. The sexual act, being pleasurable and giving a feeling of ecstasy, was considered to be what the gods themselves constantly enjoyed and therefore a 'Gift of the Gods'. Followers of the Old Religion also believed that the gods were happy to see humans happy. Actually, sex is the supreme sacrament – the union of opposites and an exemplification of the Great Work.

During the last two thousand years, the West in particular has been conditioned to believe that, without marriage, the sexual act was sinful if not worse. And, even when people were married, sex was solely for the propagation of children. A woman, however, can only become pregnant during a few days of her entire monthly cycle, but is capable of enjoying sexual inter-course, apart from her menstruation time, for the entire month. Did that mean a married couple could only have sex those few days of every month, when the female was almost sure to conceive? Yes, I'm afraid that *was* the idea. And, as you can imag-ine, this doctrine brought much unhappiness and frustration and was completely at variance with earlier pagan thought.

Sexual rites have been practised by many different and diverse occult societies the world over. However, the words 'sexual rites' imply something very different from ordinary sexual activity. The inclusion of the word 'rite' means that the act is performed for a special purpose – a special magical purpose – and that the participants are not engrossed or taken over by the act itself. At such times, the sex is of secondary importance, the mind being focused upon the *reason* for the rite and controlled by the magical imagination.

Now, unless a person can function in a higher sphere of thought while thus engaged, this type of magic is not for them. That is why sexual rites are not generally discussed in the Craft; the knowledge of them is only given to witches who are advanced enough, and indeed experienced enough, to under-stand them. When they *are* performed, it is usually between two people who are already in love and are working partners, or husband and wife. Rites of this nature are conducted when the couple are alone in the Circle, or in their own sacred space. The symbolism of male and female, positive and negative, the God and the Goddess, runs throughout the Craft and its rituals, in order to emphasise the Divine Duality.

Other reasons why sexual rites in witchcraft are not common knowledge is because they could attract the wrong type of person, or someone who is looking for sex on the cheap, or worse. Then there are those witches, or so I have heard, who although holding no allegiance to the Christian Church still have a similar cast of mind. They are found to be uncomfortable with some of the customary and proper ways of Circle procedure. This is what Gerald Gardner knew and often discussed with Arnold and me: 'I had to water them [the rites] down, you know. They just wouldn't understand the old rites, so I only give them to witches like yourselves. It's a damn nuisance, as so much could be done with the old ways of working.'

The renaissance of witchcraft with its ritual nudity as a magical practice was enough to bring the wrath of the Christian Church, not to mention the Bible-bashers and the fundamentalists, down upon the witches' heads. In the 1960s and 1970s, I had many a heated debate with churchmen on the subject, both on radio and elsewhere. Nudity in most people's minds links with sex, not least because it was taught that the naked body was sinful and abhorrent – even dirty. So modern witches were accused, as in olden times, of horrible sexual orgies. I used to point out that most naked bodies are unattractive and not likely to rouse the passions of anyone, whether in a magic circle or not. A person is much more pleasing and inviting when wearing alluring apparel, which is one of the reasons why clothing was invented.

Today, the Christian Church no longer has the power to interfere in people's lives and young folk especially, have their own codes of living and pay little attention to Christian doctrines. This is mainly because the world is entering the new Age of Aquarius, when those souls who are free thinkers have their own ideas of morality. This does not make them 'sinners' in any shape or form; they are merely tuning in, either knowingly or not, to the vibrations of the New Age.

Do the God and Goddess have to be invoked with Their secret names used in the Craft, or can a witch merely use intent to summon them?

To request the presence of the Gods, one must be courteous and also respectful, using a suitable prayer and calling Them by the secret names. The Gods are never called through an invocation: you cannot command Them to do anything. They are requested to be present through traditional methods, which include special prayers. The Wand is the proper instrument to use for this, or sometimes the Cup, depending upon the nature of the rite to be performed. I do not think that intent is enough for what should be a reverential supplication, and the very fact that special names for the God and Goddess exist within the Craft reveals the proper way to approach Them.

It is an entirely different matter when a witch experiences a vision of the Goddess or the God during meditation, sleep or at any other time. This is a purely personal experience and will occur for a very special reason. That a deity has deigned to appear to a person in this manner is extremely prophetic and will doubtless concern their future: surely something to be joyful about. These manifestations are remembered and treasured for all time.

Is it ethical to work magic to influence political outcomes or opinions?

This question infers that politicians are honest, truthful and just, and I'm afraid that is hardly ever the case. Decisions are often made which do not always benefit the country or the people they are supposed to represent, so I do not consider politics to be an unqualified example of infallibility. Therefore, I certainly believe it is ethical to work magic to influence political decisions, if by working magic you can rectify or alter existing circumstances which are against the democratic rights of the people. I must also add that in times of great dangers and peril, such as the planned invasions of Britain by the Spanish Armada and Hitler's Operation Sea-Lion, defensive magic was indeed employed for the protection of these islands.

The gift of knowing how to work and practise magic has been granted to many people who follow the old ways, and to believe that it is merely to be used for mundane purposes, such as obtaining a nice new flat for Auntie Ethel, would be an insult to this great and beneficial offering of the Gods.

Patricia, what do you do when a magical ritual does not work? I am asking this as a bona fide member of the Craft, somewhat at a loss as to what to do next, having experienced this anomaly.

I have known this to occur very occasionally, and there are a number of possible reasons for it. Firstly, if working in a coven, much depends upon the concentration and intent. Are the other witches as interested in what you want to achieve, or not? Because it only needs one person who lacks the necessary enthusiasm for obtaining a successful outcome to a working for it to fail. Of course, any magical work is usually discussed and agreed upon before a meeting takes place but, even so, there could be one or even two members who, although they concur, do not have the same commitment as the rest. These witches should be honest and admit it, so that the work can be done solely by those who really desire to do it. Jean MacDonald told me that this was the main reason why her grandmother worked only with her husband and with Jean, herself. She had reached such a high state of proficiency and did not want it to be spoiled in any way. Her grandmother also thought that introducing new people to the Craft usually brought trouble.

Another reason for a magical working to miss the mark is one of focus. Unless the focus for your magic is upon a definite and reliable objective, it will fail. And working upon a roughly associated link with what you require will also prove fruitless. You must find the actual focus that will bring results.

For example, some years ago the Sheffield coven was very keen to initiate a series of magical workings to help the 'dancing' bears in Greece, the object being to free them from the cruelty they were suffering. We knew it was against the country's laws to use bears in this way, but that if the police confiscated the animals they had nowhere to put them. So what could be the best focus for this work? The bears were kept in different places throughout Greece, and no single individual or group was responsible for their plight. It was a difficult problem which the coven discussed on numerous occasions without finding a solution. And every member expressed their concern for the bears and was eager to do something about the matter. Then I heard about Libearty, formed within the World Society for the Protection of Animals, to help bears in all parts of the world and which had turned its attention to the bears in Greece. Why not focus our magic upon Libearty and give them a boost of magical power to succeed in their task? We decided that this was the best focus for our work, if not the only one.

Sure enough, a sanctuary was built in Greece where the rescued animals were installed. They received the necessary veterinary attention for their numerous wounds, and only a few had to be put down. Many of them were eventually released into forests far away from danger, and Libearty was able to continue their work in Turkey and have recently entered India. So, I think we can safely say that the prodigious series of magical workings undertaken by the Sheffield coven over a period of several months helped to achieve a successful result.

Witches are taught that they must use their nerve power and give it to the gods, as the gods cannot help man without the aid of man. In other words, it is a two-way operation. Witches work with the Moon's power and the Moon is the ruler of the Astral Plane which is aqueous and plastic and the receptacle for most magical thought-forms. And in the course of time, are received again by the Earth.

So the phases of the moon, the Four Tides of the year, and the Mansions of the Moon should be examined to calculate the most advantageous time in which to initiate a major magical working or a new magical current.

You must also be very precise regarding the words you use during a working. Be sure that they are *exactly* expressing your goal. The words should also form a short sentence which rhymes so that, when they are repeated over and over again, they begin to say themselves and eventually become nonsense to the witches who are chanting them. All this allows the mind to concentrate more effectively upon the objective of the rite while circumambulating the Circle.

Of course, there are many different ways of working magic. Those concerned with healing for example, when contemplation and meditation can be combined with the sound of a running brook, and/or the Water Spell (see *Lid off the Cauldron*, 'Making Magic'). During these kind of rites, the atmosphere in the Circle is one of tranquillity and the power which comes not from *doing*, but from *being*, and from the concentrated effort of *willing*.

Healing work should be undertaken only with the full approval of the one to be healed. And, as Gerald said, 'You have to know what particular part of the person you want to heal, and fix that very firmly in your mind.'

A magical operation may not come to fruition if in some way it is against the Will of the Goddess, nor if the intent, however well meaning, would not entirely benefit the person concerned. The work may relieve some anguish or worry that a coven is trying to lift, but would interfere with the person's karma. Therefore, it is better that they endure their situation and overcome it themselves, rather than face a similar situation in the future. Because as most occultists realize, a karmic debt has to be repaid *alone*, and in full.

Patricia, do you think that it is more beneficial to have a 'magical partner' who is also your wife, husband or lover, or do you feel it should be someone with whom you are not personally involved?

If a witch has a 'magical partner' they are very lucky! In the 1960s they were as difficult to obtain as hens' teeth. This was mainly because many people were initiated whose partners were not interested in the Craft. I was fortunate in that Arnold Crowther (who became my husband) was an old friend of Gerald Gardner's and as deeply committed to the Craft as I am.

In order to work together, the two should be married or be lovers; this is essential. They must be emotionally involved to be a Perfect Couple and practise together. The rites of the Craft are such that, for them to be enacted properly and fully, it is necessary for the couple to be close on every level. Anything less would not achieve the required results. A man and a woman who share a friendship *can* work magic together, but not nearly so effectively.

It is said that in far-off days if the husband of a witch was not interested in witchcraft himself, she would take a male witch as her magical partner and they would be Handfasted together. And, as those witches usually kept the oaths of secrecy they took at initiation, no one was any the wiser!

Do you feel that a ritual can be successful when people from different Paths work together?

It depends entirely upon what kind of ritual is being worked. Craft rituals are performed solely by initiates of the Craft – that goes without saying – but for seasonal rituals, or any other kind, a healthy mix of people from different Paths should be invigorating and fun.

When someone is requesting initiation into the Craft, do you think that pre-study from books and initial basic training is an advantage? Or, in your opinion, is someone who is unread and without any training a better candidate as they do not have preconceived ideas?

It is very necessary for a person seeking initiation to be familiar with the basics of the Craft and with the many aspects of the Old Religion itself. A worthwhile list of books on a wide variety of byways concerning the worship of the Old Gods, and on such subjects as stone circles and sacred sites, including some sensible titles on the Craft of the Wise, should be perused.

We perform the rites from William Gray's *Seasonal Occult Rituals* for the express purpose of aiding these seekers. Through participation in these rites, they learn: the orientation of the Circle; the four basic tools – Sword (or Athame), Rod, Cup and

Shield (Pentacle); the tools' association with the Four Gates of the Circle – East, South, West and North; and not forgetting the Cord and its connection with the Spirit – the link between the Worlds. The aspirants also obtain the *feel* of working in a Magic Circle. When performing these seasonal rites, all the coven's consecrated appurtenances are removed from the altar and replaced by a separate set of tools used specifically for these rituals.

Do the Inner Rites which Jean MacDonald gave you differ from the ones we use today?

Yes, because they were always kept secret and only divulged to those witches who had gained the Third Degree. However (as Jean said), not all High Priestesses were given them; it depended upon several factors, the chief ones being a High Priestess's capacity for understanding the old ways of working magic, and how much Christian thought had intruded on their mental attitude. For the same reason many witches, during the persecution times, kept the Craft within certain members of their own families – for safety's sake. Actually, these Inner Rites contain the symbols of the First, Second and Third Degree, and thus reveal that these elevations must be passed before they are granted, if at all. Gerald knew the rites but said people would not work them today as they had been indoctrinated with the Christian mindset. Even though they might profess otherwise, if they had been born into Christian families, brought up in a Christian society, and largely taught in Christian schools, they would have been influenced by these things. Not using these rites has nothing to do with them being unwholesome or offensive in any way, merely the fact that they are different from the norm.

9 The Craft of the Wise

In witchcraft, it is only the Priesthood that is called the 'Craft of the Wise' as it contains all the ingredients necessary, on this particular Path, for a person to become a Wise One.

Long before the time of the persecutions, the Priesthood would officiate at the various celebratory festivals in the nature year. There is no doubt that they took place in the temples on hills and high places, the very sites that in the course of time the Christian Church took over for their own use.

The Craft itself was carried down with the greatest secrecy through an initiate's family and descendants – at least those members who showed an interest and were considered to be trustworthy in such matters. Jean MacDonald was one of these witches and she could trace her lineage back to at least the seventeenth century. Her greatest concern was the preservation of the old rites and, from what she wrote, it is evident that these Inner Rites were performed solely by the High Priestess, the High Priest and the Maiden. One of them is called 'Crowning the Sword'; the Crowned Sword is a symbol which appears in the Tarot and is of great antiquity. Joan of Arc – the 'Witch of Domremy' – portrayed the Crowned Sword on her personal banner. A most magical symbol indeed. Jean MacDonald drew my attention to the glyphs in the signs of the Zodiac where some of the old rites have been passed down in symbolical form. So, it is fairly obvious that at one time, these rites were widely known and practised by adherents of the Old Religion.

Not much is written about elderly witches in witchcraft books. Can you comment as to why this is?

Yes, I think so. Gerald Gardner was quite definitely an *elderly* witch and yet more has been written about him than anyone. I write considerably on Jean MacDonald who was also an elderly witch, and I must not forget that *I* am now in the same category! However, in the general context of modern witchcraft books, I agree; apart from the above witches, authors do not include elderly witches, probably because they have not heard of any. This, of course, does not mean they don't exist, rather that they prefer not to be known.

The Old Religion was always focused around kinship and the family. In early times the elderly were regarded as being the people they sprang from and having a lifetime of wisdom to impart. They therefore lived with the family and were loved, honoured and protected. When they died they were buried beneath the home or dwelling, and so were still thought of as being part of the family – the revered ancestors. Even the name 'grand mother' tells you this in no uncertain terms – the 'grand mother': not merely an old relative, but a person who was regarded with love and respect – the 'Grand Mother' or the 'Grand Father'.

I'm afraid that in today's society most old people are put into homes where they sit in chairs all day, and provided with a box which emits a variety of pictures and 'ghosts' to keep them comforted – for much the same reasons that a baby is given a rattle. Largely, they are isolated from their families and the people they love. I think it is appalling! I know that if they are very ill they cannot be looked after at home, but often they are merely old. And some old people can be very difficult – but then, so can the young! Many of these senior citizens have grandchildren (or 'grand children'), and find much enjoyment in them. Watching them at play is so rewarding to them. Witches should address this vital issue in whatever ways they can, and try to improve the lives of elder kin, and those in need. This is one important way in which the Craft can give a lead within today's so-called 'caring' society.

Some witches do not believe that the modern Craft has a continuous link with the past. Why is this, Pat?

If some witches believe this, then they are wrong. But it seems to stem from the fact that so much has been written accusing Gerald Gardner of inventing the Craft, on the basis that he brought poetry and other known pieces of literature into the Book of Shadows. Gerald intermingled these things with the original rites, ways of working etc., that he was given after his own initiation. When Gerald first talked to his peers about writing a book on witchcraft, the idea was immediately and forcefully rejected. I think he frightened them to death! Apart from anything else, there was a law against witchcraft at the time, and who knew what the Christian Church would dream up against witches, if they thought that witchcraft was still alive and kicking? This was the chief reason why the witches had dived underground for so long and had only initiated members of their own families – or at any rate, those people whom they could trust.

He wanted to compile the book to reveal the truth about witchcraft but his argument was, at best, naïve. He had discovered that what he had read about witchcraft being connected with Devil worship and the like was simply not true, and he was amazed that such an idea was still operating in the world. He was so full of enthusiasm that he wanted everyone to know the reality. He was of course, like me, a child at heart.

There was actually nothing to stop him writing such a book, except for the strictures imposed upon him by his High Priestess, Dorothy Fordham, and his Craft friend, Edith Woodford-Grimes. I very much doubt if the other members of the New Forest coven were aware of Gerald's ideas. It would not have reflected well on Dorothy or Edith for their newly initiated friend to be suggesting such dangerous things. But, as I have said before, it says much for Gerald's character in that he refrained from putting pen to paper. And it was to be several more years before his later suggestion of writing a novel about witchcraft was accepted by Dorothy and Edith because, as everyone knows, a novel is pure fiction! Thus,

High Magic's Aid was born.

Gerald has also been accused of inventing people. Notably, Dorothy Fordham née Clutterbuck, his friend and initiator from the New Forest. Professor Jeffrey B. Russell in his book *A History of Witchcraft: Sorcerers, Heretics and Pagans* states that the followers of Gerald Gardner 'tell the story that he was initiated into witchcraft in 1939 by Old Dorothy Clutterbuck, a witch of the New Forest'. He then says, 'In fact there is no evidence that Old Dorothy ever existed,' implying that Gerald had invented her, along with his initiation and the rest of the tradition of the Craft of the Wise. Well, Gerald often talked to me about 'Old Dorothy', as she was known, and I had no reason to believe he was making her up. Doreen Valiente discovered both her birth and death certificates and thus confirmed Dorothy's existence, a fact which Doreen and I had never doubted, but which was necessary to substantiate when Gerald's word had been called into question. 'The Search for Old Dorothy', by Doreen Valiente, can be found in *The Witches' Way*, by Janet and Stewart Farrar.

Most cowards attack those who have passed on and cannot answer back, but I have never known a person of Gerald's standing whose character and work has been so vilified after death. However, it does seem that no matter what is said against Gerald Gardner, or of what he is accused, he always wins. Something happens, or evidence is suddenly found, through which he is once more vindicated. Gerald always wins – even in the Summerland. And we must not forget that it was due to Gerald that thousands of people, all over the world, have found the Great Goddess and Her Consort and rediscovered their roots in the ways of the Craft and the Old Religion.

Gerald came to realize that the old ways of working magic must be preserved. That he knew of them was revealed to me when he spoke darkly of 'the old ways' during our conversations after a meeting. I agreed with him that past witches had an entirely different attitude and cast of mind. What they regarded as sacred and holy would not be so held in today's world although, happily, there are always exceptions to the rule. Also, there was no safeguard, apart from the oath, that they would be kept within the Craft. The oath should be sufficient, but over the half a century since that time we have found that it is not.

The continuous link with the past has been supported over the years in correspondence I have received from witches who had no axes to grind, and about whom I have written elsewhere. The Inner Rites which I received from Mrs Jean MacDonald two years after my initiation more than confirmed what Gerald had implied about them, and I was not embarrassed. Even Jean said that she hoped I would understand, and not think she was merely a strange old woman. I put her mind at rest. Even so, I had to promise, before the Goddess, that I would keep them secret and only pass them on to those witches who were worthy of them. A difficult task!

Jean also said that she had performed a divination on Arnold and she told me many things about him which were true, and asked me if he were a twin, which I confirmed. She said that he would also understand the rites.

What I *can* say about them is that they encompass most of the symbolism within the Craft – the Triangle, the Reversed Pentagram and the Crowned Pentagram. They also include: the artefact which purifies the soul; the ancient name of the Goddess; and the five-fold salute. The holed stone, which had been carved by Jean's grandmother for their altar, now resides upon *my* altar. And another most treasured and powerful tool I always use in ritual is the athame Jean sent to me which had been her grandmother's.

I once asked Jean if she had a rite for a coven – or knew of one. She replied to me saying that there was only one that she remembered. This, she said, used to be performed in the glades, with a feast afterwards. It was entitled, 'The Sacred Marriage of the God and Goddess', and we have performed this beautiful rite with other witches on a number of occasions. It embodies the meanings within the Second and Third Degrees and includes the symbols of those Degrees.

The name of the Goddess in this rite is 'Araeda', which I thought nothing about until an American witch pointed it out and reminded me that Gerald was supposed to have taken this name from Charles Godfrey Leland's *Aradia: or The Gospel of the Witches*. This made me look at the rite with renewed interest. Being an old lady, Jean's writing was not good, but it *was* readable, and their name for the Goddess was obviously a variant of 'Aradia'. Some time later, I discovered something else. On page 52 of Doreen Valiente's *The Rebirth of Witchcraft*, she says: 'When I first met Gerald, the name his coven were using for the Goddess was Airdia or Areda, both evidently variants of Aradia.' The second form of the name is very close to the one in Jean's rite so, despite the different spelling, you can see that this name of the Goddess has been used in covens and family groups as far apart as Inverness and the New Forest, and for a very long time – in Jean's family since at least the seventeenth century.

There is a further fascinating link with this name. In Michael Harrison's *The Roots of Witchcraft*, the author, as an expert on the Basque language, details his researches into the examination of certain old words and chants attributed to the witches. As a friend and admirer of the late Dr Margaret Murray, who had urged him to write this book, he was enraged at the way in which her literally epoch-making *The Witch-Cult in Western Europe* was dismissed: in one opinion, as 'vapid balderdash'. Harrison considered Murray to be, 'one of the most brilliant minds that this or any other period has produced'. And I agree with him, absolutely! That Murray's peers should fulminate so forcefully against her would seem to spring from what I would simply call jealousy. And add to that green-eyed monster, the book's subject matter of witchcraft, women, and the idea that witchcraft was a religion with Diana, the Moon Goddess as the deity, well, it was obviously all too much for patriarchal and prejudiced minds. But I digress.

Regarding the witch words and names, Harrison stated: '. . . one is struck by the predominantly Basque character of names at every level. . .' He discovered that the Basque name for Aradia was 'Araldia', meaning, 'the reproduction of one's kind, fertility and fruitfulness'. What better interpretation could we have for the name of the Great Goddess? Over such a long period of time and, passing through different cultures, the name could have been spelt differently, or written down wrongly. We find it today, when even in the space of a few years, a word is misspelled or misread in the process of copying it down. The important thing to remember, however, is that this name of the Goddess has been known in many different countries, and is yet more evidence of the antiquity of the witches' religion. Nearer home, the Gaelic word 'Airaidheach' means 'The lady of the Summer Pastures', while in the Highlands of Scotland when people moved away for the summer grazing, made cheeses and generally celebrated, it was called 'The Airaidh'.

Margaret Murray herself said that witchcraft must be the oldest religion in the world, and I don't think she was far wrong. The Basque people themselves affirm that their language is the oldest in the world and unrelated to any other European language. They are thought, in some quarters, to be the descendants of Cro-Magnon man – those ancient people whose artistic and telling paintings have been discovered in the deep recesses of caves in south-west France and north-west Spain. And among the paintings in these caves, a horned god and a goddess of fertility are depicted. It has been suggested that the people of the Stone Age were the first to develop any kind of language and, bearing that in mind, it is indeed awesome to contemplate that the name of the Goddess, and other witch words, could have developed from some simplistic, rudimentary sonics at the dawn of time.

Patricia, do you believe in the three-fold law of return?

In certain circumstances, yes. I believe that if you are an initiated member of the Craft and you have taken a magical oath 'to harm none', and then proceed, at some time, to perform negative magic of whatever form, then yes, I *do* think that the negative magic will

THE CRAFT OF THE WISE

rebound upon you, three-fold, because you have broken your oath. And why a three-fold law of return? Again, the answer must lie in the oath that was taken before the altar of the Goddess – *three-fold* – the Goddess Triformis. You cannot monkey about with Her. It has been found that She will exact the punishment in Her own way and really, like the Mother She is, the Goddess is teaching you the error of your ways. So, in effect, the payback goes like this: one, for the Goddess; two, for the recipient of the negative magic; and three, for *yourself*. This is how I was taught that it works.

There is also the Universal Law of Karma to consider, which most genuine witches are well aware of, and this never fails, whether or not one is an adherent of the Mysteries, or indeed any other religion or belief. If a witch performs negative magic against another person, what they are actually doing is taking *that* person's negative Karma on to themselves, presuming that the 'other person' must have acted in a hostile manner in the first place. The rule here is *do nothing* in retaliation. Sooner or later the person who has done the witch skith (harm), in any way, will receive their just rewards.

In one of her letters, Jean MacDonald wrote: 'It is harder to be a true witch than a Christian! You will find that the Goddess punishes every little error we make. Little things go wrong for us and we suddenly realize that we have done something to betray the perfect trust. It is like the Law of Karma: it never fails.'

Concerning actions good or bad that are enacted, even in a previous life, the Law of Karma can reach into a future lifetime, or the balance may be readjusted in the present life. Time would seem to be irrelevant. Decent souls who try their best to live a good life and give their help to others when it is needed are storing up plenty of positive Karma for themselves. So Karma acts both ways – it is a natural law which seeks to preserve harmony in the world.

In the Book of Shadows it states that only a young woman can become a High Priestess. Why is this, Patricia?

You must realize that in the olden days the life span was much shorter than it is today. People died from all sorts of diseases and many women died in childbirth. Life expectancy was not much greater than forty, although of course there were exceptions. Therefore, it becomes easier to understand why it was considered wise to have young women to train as High Priestesses. They would also have the benefit of being taught by a Grand Mother or Elder of the Craft – if the coven was lucky enough to have one. Chiefly, this law was a safety procedure for all concerned.

Today, if the High Priestess is fulfilling her position, there is no reason why she should not continue indefinitely. But it is still very necessary for her to possess a thorough understanding and knowledge of all aspects of the Craft. Otherwise, how can she teach her successor?

The laws in the Book of Shadows contain much commonsense (or covensense!) with respect to how a coven should be run. This is why I believe that most of them are old laws that Gerald Gardner copied down from the book which belonged to his High Priestess. It is well known that witches *did* copy Craft knowledge into their own books. Not all witches were illiterate peasants; many of the old covens contained educated people from all walks of life, who could both read and write. At Salisbury in 1653, for instance, Anne Styles was initiated and 'signed her name in a great book'.

In early times, an older witch would teach a younger one. This is how the knowledge and ways of working magic and spells were passed on. In old woodcuts and paintings, an old witch can often be seen helping a young one to prepare for the Sabbat by rubbing her body with unguents or by giving her instructions from a parchment or book. You could say that an old witch, Gerald Gardner, initiated me into the Mysteries and taught me the ways of working magic, and another elderly witch, Jean

MacDonald, gave me the innermost secrets of the Craft. But with Jean, this was not done until she had thoroughly examined my character by means of her own personal methods of divination.

The Crone is actually the most powerful, knowledgeable and wise aspect of the Goddess Triformis. And, if a witch seeks to know the answer to a problem and/or desires to be enlightened upon an aspect of the old ways, they can do no better than meditate and commune with the Crone during the time of the Waning Moon.

There is the old idea that a witch cannot die until they have passed on their knowledge to another witch – usually one somewhat younger than themselves. I believe that this is what happened in Jean's case. The gentleman who delivered her last two letters to me told Arnold that when he met her in a hotel in Spain she was wrapped up and sitting in a chair and she looked very old. I did not hear from Jean again, and presume that after passing on her secrets she entered the Summerland. I hope this answers your question as to why this law has a place in the Book of Shadows.

Regarding the Craft and its mysteries, is there any reason for secrecy today?

Indeed there is! A mystery is something which is shrouded in secrecy – otherwise, it would not be a mystery! Initially, whatever was discovered, either by accident or intent, and considered to be especially sacred or magical, was called a mystery so that it would not become common property and thereby desecrated. It would be made an important part of the tradition because of its effect and efficacy, and any worthy neophyte might discover it for themselves if they pursued their goal. Most witches are taught that magical operations must not be talked about after they have been performed, otherwise their efforts will not come to fruition. It may be said that authors, including myself, write on the subject of witchcraft while stating the secrecy aspect at the same time. That is true; but it is possible to inform the reader on many aspects of witchcraft without breaking one's oath, or betraying any secrets.

At the beginning of the revival of witchcraft, it was very necessary to debunk all the stories of Devil worship etc. in order to try and establish a saner approach to the Old Religion, and most importantly to inform society upon the reality of the Great Goddess. I for one did my best! What we didn't need was for sham witches themselves to pull it down and cause the Craft to be ridiculed and mocked.

Today, the Craft has lost some of its mystery through initiates who were either incapable of understanding the value of the Mysteries or were unable to keep their oaths. There were people like Alex Sanders, who obtained the Book of Shadows in a dishonest manner (see my autobiography, *One Witch's World*, and *High Priestess*). He also produced a record of the Three Degrees for the edification of the general public. Some other commercially minded 'witches' published the rites of the Craft in book form; but these were of value only to minds who found a prurient satisfaction in finding out (or so they thought) what witches really did. The common excuse of 'enlightening people', and 'putting everything straight', so that shadows, or even a book of them, were fully explained, was actually a futile exercise. A person could hardly initiate themselves into the Craft, and some readers must have reasoned, and rightly, that genuine adherents would not have betrayed the Craft in this or any other way.

When something is regarded as magical and potent it is said that to talk about it is the best way to lose it. This is why the Hebrews always kept the name of their god secret until the highest point of the ritual, when it was almost unwillingly pronounced by the High Priest. It was obviously a name which held great power, and so it was used with the utmost discretion, and only at the climax of the ritual.

The Four Powers of the Magus have always been considered necessary for the successful practice of magic. They are: to know, to dare, to will, and to be silent. The last Power is said to be the most important and the most difficult of the four to achieve. No loose-tongued chatterers will ever find the deepest secrets of magic. And, because the basic teachings and rituals of the Craft have been aired and become public knowledge in the present day, the innermost practices are kept more stringently secret than ever before.

Do you know anyone in the Craft who has tattoos, and are they the same as the witch's mark, or is the latter a blemish they were born with?

Yes, I know some witches who sport tattoos. A member of my coven had a little butterfly put on her bosom, which looks quite pretty, and Gerald Gardner had tattoos on both his arms. But in no way can they be described as 'witch marks'. These were most often a blemish on the skin and were what the witchfinders called the 'Devil's Mark', which they said was placed upon the body of a witch by the Devil, at his or her initiation. They may have known something about a mark that was given, but accepted anything that looked like one, as their job was to prove a person to be a witch in any way they could. The marks (or blemishes) were also known as the 'Devil's seal', or the *sigillum diaboli*. In the days of the persecutions, anyone who had a peculiar mark on their bodies could be accused of witchcraft, and probably executed as a witch. A 'witch-pricker' would strip a person naked in order to find this mark, as it was said that the Devil placed it on hidden parts of the body in order to make it difficult to find. It was also said by some prickers to be invisible and insensitive to pain, and they thought up a method of 'proving' this by the use of a trick bodkin. They would plunge the point of the bodkin into a person's flesh and be rewarded with howls of pain and a flow of blood but eventually, by sleight-of-hand, they would release the point of the bodkin so that, when it touched the flesh, it would be retracted into the handle and the victim would feel nothing. To the bloodthirsty crowd who watched the event, however, it looked as though the point had entered the flesh yet the victim had felt no pain. Ergo, they had found the Devil's Mark.

Dr Margaret Murray tells us that in many accounts of witch-craft trials, it was reported that a small blue or red mark *was* given at initiations. The application of this was thought to have been very painful, but only for a short time. We do not know where on the body the mark was given, but most probably it was somewhere on the underarm where it would be least noticeable. In this area of the body, of course, the skin is very sensitive. I mention the underarm because, as I write, this part of the body suddenly flashed into my mind. Feasible, but not proven!

There is also evidence that three 'marks' were given to initiates of the Craft on different occasions (upon their elevations through the Degrees?); the older witches, however, were the only ones to have all three, and they were the most powerful in the magical arts.

Another, more damning indictment of being accused of witchcraft was the extra nipple or 'witch's teat'. This was supposed to have been given to a witch by the Devil, in order for her to feed her familiar. Anything that looked like a teat, such as a large wart, would have condemned a person – male or female. Now, I know a witch who has exactly this type of wart on the side of his stomach. It is a little pointy thing with a tiny brown ring round it. I'm afraid he would have definitely perished if he had been caught in those days. Supernumerary nipples can occur on the human body and are recognized by medical science, but they are extremely rare.

Patricia, what do you look for as essentials in Wiccan/coven leadership?

The High Priestess must have a willingness and an enthusiasm for the position, because it entails much hard work and dedica-tion. Consequently, good leaders of covens don't grow on trees! Seriously, they must be well versed in all aspects of the Craft, as they will be expected to answer all the questions put by their members. I would look for the basic qualities of leadership, i.e. intelligence, honesty, fair-mindedness, a good sense of humour and a pleasant personality. Hopefully, the High Priestess will

1. At Carr P. Collins gathering of occultists at the Savoy Hotel, London (1981). From left – Ron Cook, the author, Doreen Valiente and Ian Lilleyman (Author's collection)

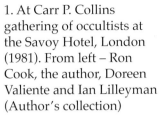

2. Edith Woodford-Grimes (DAFO), Gerald Gardner's friend and magical partner (Photo: By courtesy of Philip Heselton)

3. 'Scrying is a very worthwhile exercise to perform in the Circle' (Photo: J. Edward Vickers M.B.E.)

4. Ian Lilleyman, at Donna Gardner's grave on the Isle of Man

5. Stone carving of the 'Green Man' on a building in Sheffield (Photo: Michael Doherty)

6. Flower vase for use in Aphrodite's temple at Paphos (George Riley Scott, *Phallic Worship* 1966)

7. Stone carving on a building in Sheffield, thought to be 'Flora' – the Goddess of Spring (Photo: Michael Doherty)

8. Chalk goddess from Grime's Graves Neolithic Flint Mines in Norfolk

9. An unfinished painting by Gerald Gardner which, although unnamed, speaks for itself! (Author's collection)

10. The unmarked grave of Gerald Gardner in Tunis

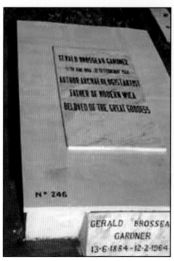

11. After the placement of a gravestone with epitaph, summer 2007

12. 'The Magician', a painting by Gerald Gardner (Author's collection)

What is Gerald Gardner Like? Arnold Crowther solved the Mystery!!!

13. Arnold Crowther's original cartoons of Gerald Gardner depicting how various people saw him. As seen by William Worrall, manager of the café at the Witchcraft Museum on the Isle of Man

14. As seen by the people of Castletown, Isle of Man.

15. As seen by the folklorist, Christina Hole

16. And by the Christian church!

have been well tutored and will realize that when a difficult situation arises in her coven, she must immediately commune with the Goddess and find the best way of alleviating it. Of course, experience is only gained through trial and error, but her High Priest should always be on hand to help in the matter.

The leader of a coven must be seen to be the leader and stand no nonsense in the Circle. But, if she is wise, she will be able to control any insubordination by accompanying her orders with a smile or an amusing remark. She must learn to be the mistress of diplomacy.

What are your pet peeves, Patricia, and where does your emphasis lie (religion, magic, healing)?

I loathe to see the Craft degraded in any way whatsoever, and I'm afraid it has been in some quarters. Today, we have no end of DIY witches, and some of their stupid actions reflect badly upon the genuine traditions of the Craft and bring it into disrepute. I understand that modern trends permit anything and everything but, when I read books in which the authors actually state that you can use your finger instead of the athame to draw the Circle, I can hardly believe what I am reading. Do they transfer the symbols on the athame to their fingers? Do they use a different finger for a wand? It is glaringly obvious that they know nothing about the true meanings and use of the athame. The writers are either pulling the readers' legs – hard – or insulting their intelligence.

Could there even be a more sinister reason behind it all? Is it yet another way of attempting to sabotage the Craft, and is this the thin end of the wedge? What comes next? Will the other sacred tools become obsolete too – even the Craft itself? But I am sure that, although there are these flaky types about, there are many thousands of rational adherents who will carry the Craft forward, intact, for posterity. They are well aware that it is the *will* of the operator which is important, and that the magical tools are an extension of the will. They are also symbols of the elements and *that* which lies behind the elements, and so are an important part of Craft procedure.

I think that the real reason behind these effete attempts to alter established methods of working is a certain disaffection, even jealousy, for the ancient Craft of the Wise and its present-day initiates. Remember the adage, 'divide and conquer?'

Regarding the second part of your question, as a consecrated High Priestess of the Goddess, my motivation has always been service to my deity. Everything else follows from that. As I stated to my initiator, the High Priest and Elder, Scire, forty-eight years ago, 'I wish to learn in order to serve'.

In a coven of such longevity we have experienced the passing of some of our oldest members and/or those who eventually formed their own covens. The mystery of death is, after all, the impetus behind religious belief, but in the Craft we are fortunate indeed to learn and experience things of the spirit and of the spiritual life which are not given to everyone.

Are you still an active teacher, Patricia?

At eighty-one years of age I am not as active as I used to be! I still attend coven meetings of course but, although most people express disbelief when I tell them my age, I am not anxious to take on any more newcomers. When anyone approaches me who wishes to be taught, I introduce them, if they are agreeable, to another High Priestess or High Priest who has hived from the Sheffield coven and has started their own. Nevertheless, I still give lectures and/or talk to people on a one-to-one basis. Witches from all parts of the world come to see me and in the course of our conversations may ask me to clarify certain aspects of the Craft. Requests to write articles or give interviews also keep me busy. And, in my professional capacity, I still perform the occasional magic and marionette show – to keep my hand in!

Since Wicca is regarded by many as a priesthood, what do you see as a child's place in the Craft?

As the Craft is indeed a priesthood and most British covens do not initiate anyone under the age of twenty-one, it is obvious that it is no place for children. However, there are many ways in which children can be taught about the God and the Goddess and about Nature. Parents in the Craft often devise simple stories, prayers and dances, and there is an excellent book on sale with pictures of the Old Gods in woodland settings, which children can colour in. Although there are ceremonies such as 'Wiccaning', when a baby is presented to the Old Gods, this does not mean that the child has to grow up to be a witch. That is something for the child to decide when it has grown to adulthood. Freedom of thought, conscience and religion has always been a basic right in democratic countries like Britain – which incorporates the three colours of the Goddess – red, white and blue – in its national flag, popularly known as the Union Jack.

How does a witch obtain a familiar?

There are different kinds of witches' familiars. One is a discarnate entity – the spirit of a person who has died. Another is a nature spirit, an elemental; and a further kind is a small animal such as a cat or a dog, or even a reptile like a toad. So the methods of obtaining any of them vary considerably.

The witches of old, especially those living in Britain, would take the kitten of a wild cat and make it their own, as this was an animal of the wild and therefore the closest to Mother Nature. To make a psychic link with the animal and to reinforce and strengthen the tie between the two of them, she would give it a drop of her own blood from time to time. As a wild animal, it would naturally regard any strangers as enemies and treat them accordingly. But to the witch, it would be malleable to any training she thought fit.

Mostly, a witch would use an animal of this kind to help her in

COVENSENSE

divination. She would cast the Magic Circle and invoke the Old Gods, then tell them what she wanted to know. She would then lay out certain objects on the ground, such as rune stones, or her own particular divinatory system, and watch what the cat would do with them. The objects the cat touched and those which were ignored or spurned by a flick of its paw would determine the answer to the witch's question. A particularly clever animal could also be used as a medium between this world and the next, and as a 'messenger' to convey certain influences to another person. This type of familiar was always loved and well cared for and given a special magical name and if its owner died it was usually passed on to another witch.

Witches who worked alone were a law unto themselves, and some of them were not too worried about using somewhat grey or negative magic to secure their ends. In 1618 a witch was hanged at Lincoln for using her cat-familiar in the following way. For some reason, she wanted to deprive the Earl of Rutland of children. She told the authorities that she had caused his existing offspring to sicken and die by stealing some of their underclothes and rubbing them against the fur of her cat, as well as conducting other magical rituals. And to prevent any further children being born, the witch had obtained some feathers from the bed of the Countess and rubbed these on the body of the cat.

There are allusions to these familiars in many of the witchcraft trials. The word 'familiar' comes from the Latin *famulus*, which means an attendant, and during the Civil War in England the Cromwellians accused the Royalist, Prince Rupert, of owning one. The animal in question was Prince Rupert's little white dog called Boye. The accusation was delivered quite seriously, and reveals that the belief in such creatures was still regarded as factual by most of the population – this, despite the established religion of Christianity and its hatred of anything smacking of magic. The accusations, however, were well and truly ridiculed and debunked by the Royalists in their pamphlets.

Many years ago, a High Priest of the Craft from London brought me a gift in the form of a print on wood of a painting by

Nicolas de Largillièrre entitled 'La Belle Strasbourgeoise'. The original picture was painted in 1703 and, in recent times, was sold at Sotheby's to the City of Strasbourg for £145,000. The Belle of Strasbourg is depicted in a lovely gown of velvet and lace and is holding a small dog which has the appearance of a King Charles spaniel. The lady is beautiful but the most unusual feature of her apparel is the hat she is wearing. It is black and of an extraordinary width: somewhat like the hat of the Magician in the tarot. A magical hat? It would seem so. My friend drew my attention to the wording on the back of the portrait: 'The Witch, "Isabelle", and her familiar "Fleur", known to the world as "*La Belle Strasbourgeois*", by Largillièrre'. So here was a lady of note who practised magic and also had a familiar. Another slight indication of her activities could be the necklace she is wearing: of equal-sized pearls and resting at the base of her neck, it resembles those worn by female witches in the Circle.

The toad was very popular with witches as a familiar, the natterjack, or walking toad, especially so. When not needed for any magical work, they were placed in the garden as they feed upon all kinds of insects and so are able to keep down those pests which threaten certain plants and flowers. The toad was usually kept in a little crock in the living-room and in suitable conditions: they have to keep their skin moist in order to breathe through it and if it becomes too dry, they will die.

Toads make good pets; they cannot bite as they have no teeth and they have the most beautiful jewel-like eyes. Apart from its participation in divinatory procedures, the toad was also valuable in connection with different types of healing. When the amphibian becomes too warm, it exudes a milky-white fluid from its skin which was called toad's milk. The witch would take this off with a little cloth and keep it for her own purposes. If used in the wrong way it is a deadly poison, but today's scientists have discovered that it also contains a substance which can be incorporated with other drugs and used as a remedy for certain eye troubles. Further, it has the properties of an hallucinogenic drug which has been named 'bufotenin'. We can only guess what the old witches used it for!

Another kind of familiar is the spirit of a person who has died. Some magicians would try to entrap such a spirit for their own purposes by various rituals which I do not propose to discuss here. It was a vile and awful procedure and one which is best forgotten. It has been known for a spirit, of its own volition, to draw close to a living person in order to give aid at a particularly distressing time in the person's life. Often, this aid will occur during sleep, when reassuring thoughts and hopeful visions of the future are introduced, so that the person awakes with the certainty that he or she is being watched over and helped from higher realms, which is indeed true.

In the witch trials, certain women stated, under torture, that they had a familiar from the spirit world who appeared to them like a living human being and they described how the ghost was dressed, down to the smallest detail. One such case was that of the Scottish witch Bessie Dunlop, whose familiar was that of a man who had been killed at the Battle of Pinkie in 1547. He told her that his name was Thome Reid and from her description of him, his ghost, with regard to its form, appeared to have been very substantial. This would indicate that Thome's astral body was still intact and his interest in earthly things undiminished.

Thome sent Bessie to see his son and gave her all manner of errands to perform for him. In return, he taught her different methods of healing the sick – both humans and animals, how to find stolen property, and other beneficial ways, both mundane and magical, of helping herself and others. But eventually Bessie was condemned and burnt in 1576. The full details of the trial can be found in Sir Walter Scott's *Letters on Demonology and Witchcraft*.

Elemental or nature spirits can also be used as familiars by magicians and witches, and are said to help them in various ways. Although belonging to realms other than the physical, they are much more elusive than other kinds of familiar and are usually contacted by means of the emotions and thought patterns.

Nature spirits can be divided into at least four categories: those that live in water are known as undines; the ones who live in fire are salamanders; the unseen spirits of the air are called sylphs; while those who reside in the earth are recognized as gnomes. Many ancient altars were raised to these spirits, mostly in lonely woods and glades, or in caves or crevices near the sea – anywhere that was considered to be close to their environment, as these spirits were petitioned to perform tasks; answer questions, or help in some other way.

The sign of the upright Pentagram is used to invoke elementals as it represents the Four Elements, plus the Spirit. It is the sign of the 'Endless Knot', and as such informs these intelligences that a higher influence is present which it would be sensible not to ignore.

The entities enshrined in trees are different from the nature spirits in that each one is the soul or spirit of a particular tree and, in my view, grows with the tree and is an integral part of it. These elementals can best be contacted by becoming a friend to a tree: touching and embracing it and letting it know that you care for it. There are many different ways of contacting such an elemental and perhaps feelings of friendship and love for a tree are among the best.

I have noticed that it is often men who attack the Craft – even those who profess to be adherents. Why is this?

I have come across this kind of antagonism many times, having been on radio programmes with Churchmen and other kinds of Christian leaders. Believe me, they loathe the very idea of a goddess – and as for worshipping one . . . And you will never change their patriarchal ideas which are so firmly entrenched in their minds. When the Church finally allowed women to be ordained they called them 'women priests', even though there is a perfectly respectable feminine noun for 'priest' which is 'priestess'. This word, they will not use. So yes, they will attack or ridicule the Craft whenever the media, or anyone else, ask them to comment upon it.

Deep down, there is still opposition in various quarters to the recognition of the feminine principle in godhead. The three great patriarchal religions have been dominant for hundreds of years, and have controlled women in a number of horrible ways, especially within their ecclesiastical ranks. And we know what happened during the persecution times. The subjugation of women has left its mark in the psyche of many men, most of whom have grown up with this teaching and all its connotations.

Years ago, I was in the company of a Catholic priest who was informed of my allegiance to the Goddess. He smiled and said, 'What a waste for Christianity'. This back-handed compliment inferred that the Church's real interest lies in converting people to Christianity – and behind that interest, of course, lies *power*. Today, that power is gradually breaking down and many people are no longer willing to be bullied or cajoled into entering a religion based upon fear. The stories that were once believed of Heaven and Hell and punishments such as burning forever in a bottomless pit have also lost their power to intimidate even gullible minds.

But where did all this hatred for the female and the feminine deity come from? To answer this question we have to go back to the very beginning of things. Archaeologists have now traced the worship of the Goddess to Neolithic times, around 7000 BC, and some to the upper Paleolithic cultures about 25,000 BC.

Goddesses have been worshipped all over the world, but it was in the Near and Middle East where both Judaism and Christianity were born, that belief in a female deity also flourished and had grown into an established widespread religion of the people.

We now sweep forward to Old Testament times, and scholars are generally in agreement that what they call the Yahwist account came into being about 1000 BC. Biblical stories of what we have been told as taking place 'in the beginning of time' have to be taken with a large pinch of salt! Much of what was written actually occurred well within recorded periods of history. Abraham, the first prophet of the Hebrew-Christian god, Yahweh, or Jehovah, arrived, most Bible scholars believe, no earlier than 1800

BC and, although the ancient Goddess religion was persecuted for centuries by those who believed that the male deity was supreme, the people still pursued their natural habits of visiting the temples of the Goddess and performing their rituals.

A certain group within the Hebrews, although standing somewhat apart from them, were the curious Levite priests said to be descended from the tribe of Levi, one of the twelve sons of Jacob. They gradually became more powerful, until only Levites were considered to be acceptable for the priesthood of Yahweh. Their status, and that of their families, was regarded as being of the greatest significance. And, as might be expected, these Levite priests became so consumed with hatred towards the Goddess religion that they compiled new laws in which they commanded the Hebrews to murder everyone in their families, including their own children, if they did not worship Yahweh. Everyone, in fact, except the husband! The Goddess religion – in which women owned their own property, had a legal identity, and could express themselves sexually – had to go. Women had to be taught that to lie with more than one man would bring vengeance upon them from the almighty. It was however accepted that their husbands could have sexual encounters with as many as fifty women, if they so desired. Nevertheless, despite the newly applied patriarchal laws, Hebrew men and women still continued to worship the Queen of Heaven. In Deuteronomy 2:33 it says that the Israelites put to death for worshipping the Goddess every man, woman and child in at least sixty cities. Under the leadership of Moses, they were told to keep for themselves every woman who had not had sexual intercourse.

It can also be seen that the myth of Adam and Eve was evolved to suppress the female religion – and the hitherto prominent position of women themselves. The Goddess had always been associated with a sacred tree. It was known as the 'Living Body of Hathor on Earth', and to partake of its fruit was to partake of the flesh and fluid of the Goddess. This sacred tree was the Near Eastern *Ficus sicomorus*, or the sycamore fig. Unlike the common fig tree, its fruit grows in dark clusters, similar to grapes. But in this new myth of Adam and Eve, the serpent (or snake), synonymous with the Goddess as an aspect of Her wisdom and of Her oracular rites, became the creature which corrupted Eve and ostensibly the whole world.

In Christian countries, the subjugation of women has continued down the ages, and been upheld by rulers, governments, universities and schools, in obedience to the doctrines of the Christian Church – that bastion of male supremacy. It was only in the twentieth century that women started to rebel against these doctrines and to challenge them.

Regarding adherents of the Craft who attack it: they usually do it surreptitiously by repeating the worn-out and incorrect statement that the Craft is a new religion with no links with the past. A particularly abhorrent form of attack is by writing personal things about Gerald Gardner, and about things which are supposed to have occurred during Craft meetings in the Circle. Although these revelations are mainly meaningless trivia, the culprits are of course breaking their oath. In my opinion, the lowest form of attack is to pick on a victim who has died and cannot answer back. I firmly believe that these private and petty disclosures are only made in order to give some kind of importance to the perpetrators. In actual fact, what they are really doing is informing readers that they are totally untrustworthy and not fit to be members of the Craft. Fortunately, these traitors are few.

I have heard you described, Patricia, as Gerald Gardner's spiritual heir. I think this epithet fits you perfectly but, on a mundane level, how did you feel when the media focused its attention upon you as well as on witchcraft generally?

Having been in the theatre for most of my life, it was nothing new or exciting for me to appear before an audience, and I agreed to give talks and to be featured in programmes on radio and television whenever I was asked, chiefly, because these were excellent opportunities for introducing the Goddess to a public that was totally ignorant of Her existence. However, with the newspapers, one had to be more circumspect and careful to whom one talked. Very careful indeed! Someone once sent me a photocopy of a front-page article from *The People*, a Sunday newspaper which appeared in the late 1950s. It concerned the Bricket Wood coven which operated in Gerald's witches' cottage in the grounds of the Five-Acres Sun Club near St Albans. The article was in the worst possible taste, with references to black magic, nude rituals, and all the rest of the ideas of a witches' coven held by the gutter press. I thought the members of that coven would have been a little more discerning about which newspaper they contacted, if they wished to publicize themselves. After that disaster, they must have decided that discretion was the better part of valour, and retired from the wicked world!

Of course, to come out and say you were a witch in those days was not an admission for the faint hearted. Neither was it sensible to be taken in by promises of a 'fair-minded' article written by the fourth estate. Many witches lost their occupations and their livelihoods, and some never recovered their status in society.

A particularly vile series of articles on the Craft appeared in the *News of the World* in February 1969. Leaders of the Craft were featured with accompanying photographs. They had all given interviews to the reporters, which were quoted at length, with many references to sex, nudism and the Third Degree. The first article featured Madge Worthington, who ran a coven at Chislehurst, Kent, and was formerly an initiate of Ray Bone. She was coupled in the paper with a Father Basil Prendergast, a then-practising Roman Catholic priest who said he was also a witch and was busily preparing to conduct the most horrific of all witchcraft ceremonies – the Black Mass. Apparently, he had been a member of Mrs Worthington's coven but had been kicked out because some of her members did not like the idea of a Catholic priest being one of them. Quite right, too!

Here, I must explain that around three years previously Prendergast had come to see Arnold and me. He turned up out of the blue one evening in an agitated state and more or less begged us to listen to his story. And what a story. It was quite a shock when he took off his scarf to reveal a clerical collar. He told us much the same story as the one in the article – that he really worshipped the dark forces and that he wanted to be a High Priest in order to conduct this Black Mass. He said that he had been in Australia working for the Church but had fallen in love with a nun who had betrayed him to the head of her convent. He was sent packing, and the sister in charge told him that, if she set eyes on him again, she would emasculate him herself. Well, all that was really quite enough for one night's conversation, so we put him right about his misconceptions concerning the Craft, and sent him on his way. We heard nothing more of him until we read these newspaper articles. Later, on the jungle telegraph, it was said that Prendergast had had some sort of accident and had been sent to Ireland.

As for Prendergast's information on the Craft, it was totally inaccurate. The Black Mass is supposed to be a parody of the Christian Mass, and to turn it into a Satanic rite the person doing it would have to believe in transubstantiation. To a person who did not believe that the wafer and the wine changed into the body and blood of the Christ, it would be complete nonsense as nothing could be achieved by insulting a piece of bread. This aberration arose within the Christian Church itself, and the Black Mass could only be performed by an unfrocked priest – i.e. one of the clergy themselves. It certainly has nothing to do with witchcraft – ancient or modern.

The following Sunday's article was headed, 'Witchcraft puts their little girl in Peril', and featured Olwen and Loic Wilson from their home in the Isle of Man. They, too, freely gave interviews to two *News of the World* reporters, who posed as would-be recruits for their coven. As such, they were welcomed with open arms and introduced to the couple's eleven-year-old daughter, Yvette. Loic was quoted as saying: 'We initiated Yvette into the Wicca when she was only four. She has only gone through the first degree so far. We will wait for another year to put her through the second and then hope that she will choose a nice witch by the time she is eighteen so she can go through the third.' The article states that they were drinking sherry and Mrs Wilson said, 'I think we ought to take our clothes off in case we decide to hold a meeting later on,' and proceeded to disrobe.

The reporters were eventually taken into the Circle where a mattress was placed before the altar. According to the article, they were both initiated, the event being described in much detail, and the following night attended another meeting with a female member of the Wilsons' coven. The lady was the wife of a hotelier on the island, whom they visited the next day. The entire article was couched in the muck-raking terminology which, at the time, made me sick to my stomach.

More exposures followed. The next one was headed, 'Witch child: police act!' but mostly concerned other witches, including a friend of ours from London, Andrew Demaine, who had also opened his heart to the reporters. Doreen Valiente introduced him to us, and he attended one of our meetings in Sheffield. A photograph of Andrew also appeared, much to his great distress.

Andrew was far from being ashamed of belonging to the Craft, but his living depended upon his professional status which was of a very high standing and included visits to Windsor Castle. His concern, apart from the tacky article, was what his clientèle would think if they read it. Andrew died from a heart attack a few days later.

Another witch mentioned was a Covent Garden opera singer, who also spoke to the reporters. She was horrified when she was told that a picture of her, sky-clad and holding a whip, was to be printed with the article. This picture (a very nice one) was not in her possession but in that of the Wilsons and, although she consulted her solicitors and did everything humanly possible to prevent it, the picture duly appeared in the paper. This lady lost her position with the opera company forthwith, but I heard, some time later, that she had married and had a baby, and life for her was good again.

The articles continued, *ad nauseam*, for many weeks, with John Score (the late editor of *The Wiccan* magazine) being another witch who was 'caught'. I cannot imagine how genuine witches could have been so naïve as to think they would be treated fairly in this type of newspaper. They should all have known better.

Alex Sanders was mentioned amongst these exposures of black magic, but that was not surprising as he was hardly ever out of the gutter press and was always spouting some ridiculous nonsense. The *Manchester Evening News*, dated 8 April 1971, carried a report of an act to be staged by Alex Sanders at the Cabaret Club in Bournemouth on Easter Monday. It was headed 'Black Magic at Easter' and Maxine Sanders was quoted as saying: 'We shall be re-enacting a black magic rite. I shall end up naked. We are showing it merely as a warning to people not to meddle with black magic.' Needless to say, it all ended 'in tears'.

What would you like people to know about you? What would you like to pass on about the Craft?

I would like people to think of me as a person who carried on Gerald Gardner's work after he passed over, bringing the Great Goddess back into the consciousness of the human race and broadening people's minds to the idea of magic. I would like to convey to people that, by using the magical imagination, their lives could be so much more satisfactory and they could achieve much greater things than they thought possible.

When I became known in the media as a 'White Witch' (their epithet, not mine), I started to receive invitations to give talks and lectures. This is a much better way of spreading the word than by talking to reporters, who have no real interest in the subject except from a sensational angle. They nearly always write what they *think* you said, and not what you actually told them. I spoke to many different societies, clubs and universities (and still do), and also became an after-dinner speaker.

Most people are fascinated to hear about witchcraft, and they are greatly enlightened (or so they say) after hearing my talk. I really enjoy speaking, because I can tell an audience that the Craft is part of the Western Mystery tradition, something totally different from what they have hitherto believed – that it involves black magic, orgies, and that kind of thing.

I would like to pass on the fact that the Priesthood of the Craft has been in existence for many thousands of years, that it grew from the ancient religious cultures of Sumer, Babylon, Ancient Egypt and Albion, and that the priestesses of the temples passed down the magical practices when the religion of the Goddess was overthrown.

Do you continue to work with people after they have hived off to start a new coven?

Not as a rule. There seems little point in following the new group when you have your own coven to run, and I think the new High Priestess or High Priest are better going it alone, as they may be a little put off by the presence of their former leader. I have been asked to attend various meetings of a new coven and, as I had been invited, I gladly agreed. Sometimes a new leader has requested my advice on a certain matter and this is always a good sign. We learn from each other, and witchcraft is a learning system or so I have found.

There are times when members of covens which have hived from the Sheffield coven meet for the celebration of a festival or other important occasion. As I am now a Grand Mother, there have been visits from two Great Grand Daughters of my coven, three times removed from the Sheffield coven, and that is very gratifying to me.

Keeping in touch with 'relatives' is important, especially when it comes to magical workings. A large project needs all the power it can get so, at those times, several covens work at different locations, but on the same date and at the same time. Schedules are adjusted, if necessary, to coincide with different time zones.

How do you see the Craft and paganism developing in the future?

I believe that the Craft and paganism in general will have a big part to play over the coming years, especially now the world is entering the Aquarian Age. I don't see the Craft as a mainstream religion, not in the ordinary sense, at least I hope it does not achieve that doubtful privilege. I say this because, when any religion gains power over people, things begin to deteriorate: witness the Catholic Church and the horrors which are happening today as a result of patriarchal religions. Most of the horrors stem from the laws in sacred books which are believed to be God's words and instructions. This is truly terrifying! I know that the Old Religion contained legends and myths, but these were mostly concerned with the adventures of the gods, coupled with fabulous tales which held hidden truths. I have not found any which sought to control people by fear and the threat of eternal punishment after death.

In this new Age of Aquarius, it is said that every man and woman will become their own saviour. And, as each Age lasts for around two thousand years, there will be plenty of time for this prophecy to become an actuality. This prophecy is saying that there will be no avatar coming to the Earth to hold your hand and tell you what to think about the afterlife and matters pertaining to it. Aquarius is the sign of *extension* – on all levels, including that of the Soul or Spirit. Esoteric abilities will become the norm and the Spiral of Evolution will continue to draw humanity towards a much wider comprehension of who they really are. The Children of Earth will become the Children of the Stars. I believe that the Great Goddess will resume Her rightful role as the Queen of Heaven – the Star Goddess – and be recognized as such. Remember, the word for the New Age is *transformation*.

The adherents of the Craft today are already 'in tune' with these future trends, simply because many of the trends have always been a part of the Craft's teachings. For example, witches do not believe in indoctrinating their children into their own beliefs, however admirable they may be. They believe that their children, as they grow up, should think for themselves. Children need to find their own pathways in life and to weigh things up for themselves with a dose of good sound sense. Of course, their parents must guide them and tell them about the Goddess and Her Consort, and especially encourage them to care for the animals and birds, who are the Great Mother's children.

The Old Religion has survived because it is based upon ancient verities and is the faith of the free-thinker. It encompasses the need for spiritual evolution with knowledge, not fantasy of, the afterlife. It teaches an understanding of the nature year with its many masks and upholds the feminine principal in divinity. It has emerged into the light once more, to take its rightful place in the world, although it may be a long time before it is acknowledged universally; but what we have today is definitely a new beginning.

When I think of the progress which has been made over the last fifty years, and the thousands of souls who have come to know the Old Gods, it is truly amazing! But what is needed in the world, and what I hope will come to pass, is for the philosophy of paganism, with all that it entails, to be understood and acted upon. Today, one of the most important aspects in this regard is not that of saving the beauty of the world, but saving the world itself. The power of thought is very great – this is where all influences are generated for good or ill – and thoughts combined with magical force can achieve almost anything. You have been taught how to perform magic, and now is the time to use it – in this particular and crucial instance, to save the world.

Do you think that something has been lost amidst the commercialization of the Craft?

Yes, most certainly! If money is taken for instruction in Craft procedure, it besmirches and degrades the Craft and also the person who is charging the fee. We are speaking of the ancient Mysteries and of the evolution of the soul, and these things are sacred and cannot be bought. But, however much iconoclasts attempt to destroy the spiritual values of the Craft, in this way, they will not succeed. There will always be honourable initiates who will protect it from such vandals. Gerald once said that he had received a letter from a clergyman, offering £1 for a tape-recording of the secret rites. His comment was, 'Well, you know, even Judas got thirty bob!' But, aside from the above, the running costs of a study group on exoteric subjects should not be the onus of the teacher; the cost of items such as light, heating and refreshments should be shared among the students.

Patricia, have you found that there are problems when Craft initiates are married to spouses who neither practise the Craft nor approve of it?

Well, certainly not in *my* coven. If a person wishes to join the Craft, these kind of problems are sorted out well before any initiation takes place. It is very important to know if there are any objections from the person's husband or wife because if there are it would not be wise to initiate them. No good can come from it, and would-be initiates should realize this.

If something of this nature arises *after* the initiation has occurred, and when the initiate had assured us that their partner had no objections, it is better to request them to absent themselves from the coven until they have sorted the matter out. We cannot be expected to interfere in matrimonial matters, nor should we be expected to do so.

Thirteen is the number of a full coven of witches, I believe. Not being an initiate, myself, I presume this number was taken from the thirteen full moons in a year. But what would happen if fourteen or more witches were present, or is this not allowed?

It is allowed, and nothing negative would happen, but it was found that a 9-foot Circle could accommodate thirteen witches most comfortably and, as you say, the number was taken from the usual number of full moons in a year. (Occasionally, there are only twelve.) But these are not the only reasons for this number. In early times, there were also thirteen signs of the Zodiac, and a Lunar rather than a Solar calendar was observed. There is yet another reason for this number which relates to the Craft of the Wise. It is not a dark secret, but witches are supposed to be able to work the answer out for themselves!

On one occasion, the Sheffield coven did have fourteen witches in the Circle. That was when Doreen Valiente came to visit us. The Circle did not seem too crowded and we managed very well. And on that night I had a deep trance experience which I shall never forget.

Thirteen has always been regarded as a sacred and magical number. It links with the Moon which is also the symbol of the Goddess. Many kinds of societies have adhered to this number, with twelve souls plus the leader. Romulus had his twelve Lictors; Charlemagne, his twelve Paladins; Robin Hood had twelve followers, or merry Men; Jesus had twelve disciples; and even in the British courts of law, there is a jury of twelve, plus the judge.

Regarding the popular hero Robin Hood, according to Robert Graves in his book *The White Goddess*, one J.W. Walker has proved that this hero of legend was an historical character born in Wakefield, Yorkshire, between the years 1285 and 1295. The son of Adam Hood, a forester, Graves states that Robin and his outlaw band formed a coven of thirteen, with Maid Marion (his wife Matilda) taking the part of Maiden of the coven.

On a more mystical level, the number thirteen has always been prominent. In Welsh legends we find 'Thirteen Kingly Jewels', 'Thirteen Wonders of Britain', 'Thirteen Precious Things' and so on. But the Christian Church, you must agree, did its work extremely well in making people fear the number thirteen. Like everything else associated with the Old Religion, it was condemned as being evil or unlucky, and this superstition has continued right into the present day.

Friday the 13th was once considered a most auspicious day, being the day of Venus, the Goddess, combined with this sacred number. I have often been requested to attend some function on this day, such as choosing the winner of a fancy dress competition where the people were dressed as witches or wizards. Some thumb their noses at any bad luck, but nevertheless have not forgotten this date. It is still well implanted in their subconscious minds!

Christians believe the superstition arose from there being thirteen men at the Last Supper, and the subsequent ill-fated events which followed it, so would refrain from having thirteen at table, and invite another guest to avoid it. And the number thirteen is nearly always absent from hotel rooms, being changed to 12a, or something similar. Witches, on the other hand, have no such qualms knowing this sacred number's true derivation.

10 Talismans

Talismans can be anything from a nation's national flag to a tiny piece of jewellery. In the widest sense, talismans symbolize safety and protection, and/or fundamental qualities which guarantee continuance and hope. A talisman also produces an auto-suggestive sense and feeling in tune with the reasons behind its origin.

In the field of occultism, talismans are created for a specific magical purpose and are round or square pieces of metal roughly two inches in diameter. They are usually inscribed with the sigils and symbols of one of the major planets, including the kamea (magical square of numbers) belonging to a particular planet, inclusive of the Sun or the Moon. This system aligns with the occult principles of the Qabalah. Reliable sources for study can be found in *Talismans, Amulets and Charms* by Leo Vinci and *How to Make and Use Talismans* by Israel Regardie.

Alternatively, talismans can be constructed from any symbols or magical signs which are meaningful for the purpose required, and parchment is acceptable in place of metal. The knowledge concerning talismans has been derived from much earlier sources which reveal this subject's immeasurable age.

Is it really important to make and consecrate talismans at specific astrological times?

You can make talismans at any time you like, but somehow I doubt if they will be as efficacious as when they are made in accordance with fortunate astrological aspects. Why? There are many reasons, but one of the most important is revealed by Hermes Trismegistus (thrice-great Hermes), or Thoth, the Egyptian god of knowledge. The doctrine is said to have been engraved upon the Smaragden, or Emerald Tablet, and is a synthesis of the mystery of life, the foundation of astrology and magic, and an acknowledged key to alchemy. It begins, 'That which is below is like unto that which is above, and that which is above is like unto that which is below, for the performing of the miracle of the One Thing' – the One Thing being of course, *life*.

The universe and everything in it is a unity. Planets, people, animals, vegetation etc. are linked and in harmony, and there is a key which we can use to connect ourselves more closely with it, and understand it more clearly – and that key is *astrology*.

Cosmic energy and vibrations thrill through the universe, are echoed and passed to the Sun, Moon and planets – including our Earth – and affect them accordingly. These vibrations are said to link with the sacred number seven, and are often called the Seven Rays. The ancient Sumerians and Babylonians used the Seven Planets known to them, and these planets still have rulership over the seven days of the week, the signs of the Zodiac, colours, metals, stones, the hours of the day and night, the colours of the rainbow, in fact everything in Nature. The five planets and luminaries (they knew that the Sun and the Moon were luminaries, not planets) have been given names according to the gods who ruled the Seven Rays – Saturn, Jupiter, Mars, Sol, Venus, Mercury and Luna. They are the material manifestation of the Seven Rays, and the means by which the rays are transferred to the Earth.

St Thomas Aquinas (1225-74) asserted, 'The celestial bodies are the cause of all that takes place in the sublunar world', while Tycho Brahe (1546-1601) affirmed, 'Those who deny the influence of the planets violate clear evidence which for educated people of sane judgement it is not suitable to contradict'.

Although there were other planets waiting to be discovered, namely Uranus, Neptune and Pluto, their orbital paths being the furthest away from the Sun, they are thought by astrologers to encompass and influence more worldly events than the others. The effects of these planets did not begin when they were discovered; one might rather say that the discovery of these planets came at the right time for their effects to be recognized and understood. Their presence in a natal chart however, carries weight and certainly influences the person's life.

As we are the microcosm of the starry macrocosm, and in view of the above, there can be no better way to make a talisman than by attuning it to our planetary system.

My partner has asked you a question about talismans. Could I follow that up by asking if you could give me a reliable way of consecrating one and actually using it?

Gerald Gardner gave me a lot of information concerning the making and the consecration of a talisman. He made one for me when I needed some help in overcoming a negative influence which was interfering with my theatrical performances, and I am pleased to record that it worked.

Maurice Bruce, an occultist known as 'the Magician of the North', also contributed to my knowledge of talismans. One thing to remember is that, once made, a talisman can be used throughout your life, providing what you want comes within the astrological sphere in which it was made. Other talismans can be constructed with different aspects, according to what is required.

For consecration, erect the Circle, or utilize your own sacred space. Use your own words to form a short mantra thus: 'Thou creature of thy kind; thee I consecrate to my purpose.' Repeat it *seven* times. Keep your talisman as secretly as possible; neither showing it to anyone nor allowing anyone else to handle it, if this can be avoided.

Work as simply as possible at first. For invoking, use the second, third, fourth and fifth days (or evenings) of the *New Moon*. You can ask the talisman for help with almost anything provided that it is a personal need, and bearing in mind to which planet and aspects the talisman is attuned. Repeat the same wish on each of the four days at first, until you find how the talisman reacts.

If you prefer, you may use one invoking day each month, but make it the *same* day of the New Moon to maintain the twenty-eight-day cycle without interruption.

For invoking, again you must develop your own ritual but use, as a basis, something like this. Polish the talisman with plate polish and a *clean* cloth, saying something like: 'Thou creature of [name the planet], thee do I purify and awaken to life for the purpose of [whatever you want].'

When expressing your command say: 'Make clear the way for [your first name], daughter [or son] of [your mother's first name], to obtain————'

Express your wishes as the opening of a door or portal or a path, and *imagine* a door opening at your command, and picture, as accurately as you can, the state of affairs you want to bring about. *Never make a negative command.* Don't, for example, picture something you want to be rid of, and give the command for it to be banished. Always picture what you want. Include yourself in this mental picture as possessing the object or enjoying the state of affairs. A lot depends upon clear imagery.

When you begin to get even minor results make some sign of recognition by means of putting a flower in a special vase or lighting a candle on the altar. Do this as an act of *encouragement* and *recognition*.

The talisman is *not* the deity but just an intelligent instrument which performs the work under the ruling of the deity.

Don't speak of any results you get. The more secret you keep everything connected with the talisman, the more effective it will be.

Finally, keep the talisman in a velvet pouch and always hold it in clean hands.

11 The Old Religion

When witches speak of the Old Religion they usually mean the religion of the Great Goddess, the Horned God, and the pantheon of all the other pagan gods which existed in Europe and the Middle East for thousands of years. Other countries also worshipped these deities and, in parts of India and elsewhere, still do.

It seems that, despite persecution, propaganda and Christian missionaries, the Old Gods refuse to be banished. They may have been forcefully eclipsed and replaced by new gods over the course of history but, in Britain and many other countries, they are still placated and honoured in the hundreds of ancient customs, enacted without fail, every twelve months, on the appropriate day.

The Goddess and the Horned God are enshrined in the depths of the human psyche as the rightful gods of humanity, inherent in nature and the entire complexity of life itself. They were not conceived from the teachings of prophets or leaders. They were recognized as representations of the divine twin forces encompassed in all existence. This is the reason why the God and the Goddess continually reassert Themselves. They exist at the deepest atavistic level of human consciousness as the embodiment of the Infinite One – the cause of all creation.

Is there a link between horses and the Craft?

In Gwion's 'Song of the Horses', the White Goddess says:

> Handsome is the yellow horse,
> But a hundred times better
> Is my cream-coloured one
> Swift as a sea-mew . . .

The horse was considered to be a sacred animal in Britain from as far back as prehistoric times, and is closely associated with the Moon Goddess. So, yes, the white horse, particularly, has a magical link with the Old Religion and therefore the Craft.

The horseshoe is a symbol connecting the horse with the moon and it has come to mean good luck. The blacksmith is the only person who can safely turn the 'horns' downwards. He places it above his fire so that the luck will spill down on to his forge. At Stonehenge, the placing of the five separate dolmens, arranged with an opening at one end, resembles the shape of a horseshoe.

The horse was certainly sacred in the Old Religion. A very ancient rite is called 'the White Mare and Her Ninefold'. It has always been kept most secret because it *can* be dangerous if misused. In this rite, the Goddess, in the form of the White Mare, connects with the most primitive part of the brain.

The goddess Demeter was widely worshipped as the Mare-Goddess, and also under the name of Epona, or 'The Three Eponae', denoting her three-fold aspect, especially among the Gallic Celts, and in Ireland up to the twelfth century. A particularly cruel ceremony, involving the death of a white mare, took place at Tyrconnell in Ireland during the crowning of an Irish pseudo-king.

In the city of Coventry, a young girl, naked and riding a white horse, took the part of the 'Godiva' rider at the spring festival. In this pagan ceremony, the girl represented the Goddess in Her aspect as 'Maiden'. In the eleventh century, Lady Godiva also rode naked through Coventry on a white horse for an entirely different reason. Her husband, Leofric, Earl of Mercia, promised to reduce the heavy taxes on the people if she rode naked through the streets at noon. The grateful citizens remained indoors as she did so, but a man who for obvious reasons became known as 'Peeping Tom' bored a hole in his shutters and was struck blind for his pains. So goes the legend.

A British Old Stone Age piece of art was discovered in the Derbyshire Pin-hole Cave. It is a carving on bone of a man wearing a horse-mask, and is now in the British Museum.

White Horse hill-figures positively abound in Britain, from as far north as Aberdeen, down to the south coast of England. The county of Wiltshire is a veritable stable of white horses – at Hackpen, Alton Barnes, Westbury, Broad Town, Pewsey, Marlborough and Cherhil, among others. Marlborough's White Horse achieves immortality in the Marlborough School Song: 'Ah, then we'll cry, thank God, my lads, the Kennet's running still, and see, the old White Horse still pads up there on Grantham Hill.'

Many of these White Horse hill-figures were cut close to hill-forts and barrows, which again speaks of the fact that in ancient times the white horse had a definite religious significance, and always seemed to be near those who worshipped the Goddess. Curiously, the British people have an inborn repulsion of horse-flesh, and even during the Second World War, when food was scarce, refused to eat it.

In Aberdeenshire a very ancient pagan ritual used to be enacted. The last sheaf of corn reaped was called the 'maiden', and was kept until the next mare foaled, when it was given to the mare as its first food. The ceremony was named 'Calling the Mare' and, if you finished reaping before a neighbour, you threw a corn 'dollie' in the shape of a horse into their field and shouted, 'Mare'. This was to encourage the laggards as the last one to finish had to house the corn dollie for the winter, and as it was quite large, it could not be easily concealed or forgotten!

The Kilburn Horse in Yorkshire was cut by one Thomas Taylor. It appeared that he was so impressed by the Uffington

Horse, he had one cut on a hillside in his own locality. Taylor's reaction to the Uffington Horse is quite understandable. It is the most mysterious of all Britain's horse-figures and also the most ancient. It has dominated the Vale of the White Horse in Berkshire for the last 2,000 years. It is the largest of Britain's white horses, measuring 360 feet in length, and is superior to any of the others. A marvellous portrayal of a horse in motion, made with a mere five stencil-like lines, one can almost hear the sound of its hoofs pounding the turf. Its disarticulated limbs, beakish mouth and the eye are reminiscent of Celtic art, and are similar to the repoussé horses on the Marlborough and Aylesford Buckets. In 1738 the Revd Francis Wise wrote in 'A letter to Dr Mead concerning some Antiquities in Berkshire': '. . . the horse at first view is enough to raise the admiration of every curious spectator, being designed in so master-like a manner that it may defy the painter's skill to give a more exact description of that animal'.

Most of these hill-figures were scoured every seven years – the number of magic and mystery. In Berkshire, as in other counties, people arrived from miles around to help with the cleaning and scraping. An old Berkshire ballad was sung at the time:

The owl White Horse wants zetting to rights
And the Squire hav promised good cheer,
Zo we'll gee un a scrape to kip un in shape,
And a'll last for many a year.

The lord of the manor considered it his duty to feed and entertain the workers while they were at Uffington. It was a great social event too, with a fair and sports and all kinds of entertainment which lasted over three days. In the intervening years, since 1857, the scouring was forgotten, so the Horse became so overgrown that its exact position was difficult to locate. Happily, today, it is under the care of the Ministry of Public Buildings and Works and receives thousands of visitors every year. Some of them may know the secret of the Uffington Horse, which connects with its 'eye' – a large, flat stone. It is said that, to stand on the 'eye', turn round three times and make a wish, brings that wish to fruition. I can confirm that it does!

The 'eye' of the Uffington Horse is said to lie directly above a 'blind spring' – where several underground streams of water meet. Much work has been done on these underground sources of energy or water, and it is considered by major writers on the subject, including Guy Underwood, that all sacred sites, hill-figures and stone circles were erected over primary geodetic lines which are connected with germination and growth. Underwood was of the opinion that the ancient people marked these places as sacred, so they were in fact the esoteric centres of the Old Religion in more ways than one!

The following verses by G.K. Chesterton are taken from Book Five of his poetry, *The Ballad of the White Horse*, which captures the atmosphere of the place to perfection:

Before the gods that made the gods
Had seen their sunrise pass,
The White Horse of the White Horse Vale
Was cut out of the grass.

Before the gods that made the gods
Had drunk at dawn their fill,
The White Horse of the White Horse Vale
Was hoary on the hill.

Age beyond age on British land,
Aeons on aeons gone,
Was peace and war in western hills,
And the White Horse looked on.

For the White Horse knew England
When there was none to know;
He saw the first oar break or bend,
He saw heaven fall and the world end,
O God, how long ago.

For the end of the world was long ago
And all we dwell today
As children of some second birth
Like a strange people left on earth
After a judgement day.

For the end of the world was long ago,
When the ends of the world waxed free,
When Rome was sunk in a waste of slaves,
And the sun drowned in the sea.

And all the while on White Horse Hill
The horse lay long and wan,
The turf crawled and the fungus crept,
And the little sorrel, while all men slept,
Unwrought the work of man.

With velvet finger, velvet foot,
The fierce soft mosses then
Crept on the large white commonweal
All folk had striven to strip and peel,
And the grass, like a great green witch's wheel,
Unwound the toils of men.

In one of your talks I attended, Patricia, you mentioned that some altars in the Old Religion had horns at each corner. Was this the norm?

I don't know whether the altars in the great temples were thus decorated, as thousands of them were destroyed along with the temples themselves. What I was speaking about were small *domestic* altars, dating from the tenth to the ninth centuries BC, which were found at Megiddo in Palestine. Photographs of them appeared in *The Archaeology of Palestine* by W.F. Albright. They are square in shape, around two feet high, and decorated with little horns at each corner of the surfaces.

Among other aspects of archaeological interest, this book

covers the extent of Goddess worship in Palestine from as far
back as the nineteenth century BC. The figure of what is called the
'serpent Goddess' is shown on a stele where a large serpent is
encircling the body of the Goddess. It was found at Tell Beit
Mirsim near Bethlehem, and dated to the sixteenth century BC.
Small pottery plaques, mostly oval in shape, and known as
'Astarte plaques', have been excavated in abundance. Some of
them show the Goddess with Her arms upraised, grasping lily
stalks or serpents in Her hands, while Her hair is adorned with
long ringlets. Much later in time, around AD 150, in the Antonine
period, a magnificent temple was built at Gerasa in honour of
their patron-goddess, Artemis. The construction took many
decades and culminated in massive propylaea (gateways) which
were duly dedicated to the Goddess.

But to return to the horned altars. I do think it would be a
splendid idea for witches and pagans to have similar, small,
domestic altars in their homes, apart from the altars they may
have in their temples or covensteads. An enterprising craftsman
could make them from wood and, being quite small, they would
fit into any convenient corner of a room. Flowers, a candle flame,
incense, or any offering could be placed upon them, and this type
of altar, as in ages past, would be a personal and private one used
solely by its owner.

How old do you consider the Craft to be?

How long is a piece of string? Well the Craft is the Priesthood of
the Old Religion and archaeologists have placed the worship of a
feminine deity to at least 25,000 BC. Dr Margaret Murray declared
that it was the oldest religion in the world. But, regarding the
Craft *per se*, we know that the Mysteries of the Goddess were
practised in Her temples by priestesses throughout the ancient
world and that, when these temples were destroyed, the
Mysteries were handed down through the distaff line and eventually became linked with witches and witchcraft, when men
became initiates too. However, because of the persecutions, and

the later laws against witchcraft, adherents dived underground and virtually disappeared. And who could blame them? So what happened to the Mysteries? They were passed down in families and kept most secret. My friend and informant, Jean MacDonald, said that her Craft family line went back to at least the seventeenth century; not forgetting the New Forest coven, which as Dafo affirmed was an hereditary one.

Temples raised to the Old Gods in Britain on hills and high places were taken over by the Christians and turned into churches. We know this is true because, when Christianity first appeared in Britain, the followers of the Old Religion were told that they could worship their gods in these churches but that their altar would be at the opposite end of the church to that of the new religion. This was set in the east – the direction from which Christianity was born. Followers of the Old Religion had also to enter the church through the North Door, not the main door, which was usually set in the south. Now, if these churches had not been erected upon already sacred ground, and adapted from pagan temples, the followers of the older faith would have had no interest in them, nor have wanted to worship in them. There is also the matter of the North Door. Why the North Door? I believe that this was the main entrance for the original building or temple. To those of the Old Religion, the north was, and still is, especially venerated. The old altar may even have been situated in the centre of the building, rather than at one of the compass points near a wall. Certainly there came a time when the pagans were no longer welcome at all in these churches and even the North Doors were blocked up. There are literally hundreds of old churches in the British Isles where this can be seen.

Carvings of the Green Man abound in old churches, along with enigmatic faces of denizens from the netherworld which peer at you from dark corners or leer from high protruberances. The Goddess is usually portrayed as a mermaid, or more forthrightly as the fount of all life, in those carvings known as Sheila-na-Gigs, where she exposes Her vulva. These thousands of carvings must have been made with the approval of the Christian priests, who could easily have stopped the masons from making them if they had so wished. They probably realized the importance of these pagan deities; indeed a number of prelates and bishops were accused over the years of having practised witchcraft or demonology but never punished.

We now come to the *pièce de resistance* of this subject, which we owe to the brilliant work of Michael Harrison, detailed in his book *The Roots of Witchcraft*. He tells us that just after the end of the Second World War the late Professor Geoffrey Webb, Secretary of the Royal Commission on Historical Monuments, was requested to inspect 'such of England's ancient churches as had suffered damage through aerial and other bombardment'. This he did and, in one of the churches he surveyed, an explosion had moved a slab of stone which formed part of an altar-top, thus disclosing what lay within, and what had remained hidden inside the altar for many centuries. What lay within that dark recess was a symbol of the Old God – the God of the Pagans. And the form that symbol took was that of the Sacred Phallus of the God, carved in stone. Amazingly, this discovery was not an isolated one, because it gave Professor Webb an invitation to explore altars in other damaged churches. He found that 90 per cent of the churches he examined had the symbol of the ancient God concealed within the altars.

So the new religion of Christianity not only encouraged the followers of the Old Faith to enter their churches by displaying pagan symbols such as the Green Man, but actively used the power of the Old God in their holy of holies. Obviously, they thought they needed this ancient and universal image of the Giver of Life (known in India as the *lingam*) to bolster their new religion.

What other practices of the Old Religion were filched by the new clergy? We know that they had knowledge of magic and often used the darker side of this art. They performed the Black Fast to stop me from lecturing in Tewkesbury, but it failed. This negative magic involves fasting and praying for some days while concentrating the mind upon what is required. I know what the clergy did because it was reported in the press at the time. How foolish of Christian priests to admit to working magic – and Black Magic at that.

How do you think that religion came into being, and do we really need it?

This question brings to mind an excellent explanation of the word 'religion' that I recall reading somewhere. 'Religion is for those who do what they are told, regardless of what is right. Spirituality is for those who do what is right, regardless of what they are told.'

A religion implies a belief or knowledge in an afterlife and, when early humans developed a form of language and were able to communicate ideas about birth, life and death, what we now call 'religion' probably evolved. These early ideas progressed into the concept of a creative force which was generally perceived in a human likeness. And from this initial hypothesis various religions came into being, which purported to explain the reason for life on Earth.

At the beginning of human life, there would undoubtedly have been much wonder when people looked up at the stars, the sun and the moon, and at their natural environment, wherever they happened to live. The beauty and grandeur of it must have made them think that something or someone was behind it all. They would also have noticed how vegetation – the plants and the trees – came into life, apparently died, then returned to life again. One can imagine their terror when a thunderstorm occurred, or when there was a solar eclipse and they were plunged into darkness. How relieved they must have felt when the light returned once more. Almost everything around them had a rhythm of birth, death and rebirth, in an unbroken and continuous cycle, circle or spiral.

It may have been this perpetual returning of things which created the circle dance (portrayed in the masterly art of the palaeolithic cave paintings), along with sympathetic magic, in which the participants imitated, by actions, what they required at the time. This was also echoed in the artists' paintings deep within the sacred caves. The most famous picture is that which is called 'The Sorcerer' in Les Trois Frères caves of Lascaux, France, and depicts a man wearing a horned mask and the skin of an animal while performing what appears to be sympathetic magic.

The many paintings found in such caves usually portray a successful hunt, and I believe were put there to show an Earth Mother what they wanted to achieve by their magic and to gain her blessing. It is obvious, from the hundreds of diverse paintings, that the magic worked, and the brilliant execution of the animals show the care with which they were painted. In these pitch-black caverns, the exactitude of the many different animal forms reveal a necessity for perfection, or as close to it as the artists could achieve. In the lightless passages and caverns the pictures would be seen solely by the one who painted them. Such bold certainty speaks of the mystical influence in which these places were held, and a convincing magico-religious approach, where the beauty and splendour of the animals was clearly acknowledged to be sacred.

Grime's Graves neolithic flint mines in Norfolk are the largest and best known group of flint-working sites in Britain. The base of what is known as Pit 15 revealed the figure of a chalk goddess (4¼ inches high) and obviously pregnant, on a triangular heap of blocks of mined flint, with a chalk lamp nearby. Seven red-deer antlers lay on the heap, together with other ritual offerings. Evidently, the Earth Mother was recognized, and propitiated with gifts for abundant good-quality flint in the surrounding pits. Chalk phalli were also found and there is definite evidence suggesting the practice of magical ritual from at least two of the galleried pits.

Aboriginal beliefs in Australia are not only ancient but also vivid and memorable, and a testament to those people's strong attachment to the ways of their ancestors. The further a religious belief goes back, the more powerful and vigorous are its spiritual legends. The stories of later faiths are often dressed up or elaborated upon so that devotees can better understand their meanings or to keep people entertained but ignorant.

Another kind of interference came from the Christian Church which was responsible for the worst act of vandalism: that of robbing different races of their spiritual beliefs and imposing upon them the religion of Christianity, which was completely alien to their own cultural heritage and teachings. The act was performed for the Church by their missionaries who were sent to various countries to 'enlighten the ignorant' and to gain more power for themselves. The missionaries however, were unable to penetrate every country or continent on the globe, so there are still some races whose spiritual beliefs remain intact.

Early humans were also free from the Christian dictates constantly instructing them that psychic abilities of any kind were an abomination and of the Devil. Our ancestors' lives were simpler and also free from modern technology, electrical instruments such as radio and television so people's psychic faculties would have been better able to function. In their state of innocence and mental freedom, early people were instinctively aware of the spiritual dimension of being, and most probably experienced visions and apparitions of the dead.

This, then, is my opinion as to how belief in the spirit first came into existence – undisturbed by state religions and man made dogmas which, long aeons later, were to follow.

As to whether we really need religion, it depends upon what you mean by the word 'religion'. Although many people now feel that state religions have no value in the present day, it must be recognized that they have filled a vacuum without which the general populations of many countries would have been bereft of any kind of spiritual guidance. A large percentage of the populace still depend upon the state religion for ceremonies connected with birth, marriage and death, as the accustomed manner in which these ceremonies are enacted. And I feel that, although state religions are in decline, it will be a considerable time before these customs cease to exist. However, there is a noticeable and refreshing change taking place today, where individuals holding different beliefs, such as witches and pagans, are enacting their own ceremonies in public, with their own priests and priestesses. Those who have no beliefs as such, and do not want Christian burial for their loved ones, can often find an alternative officiate from the funeral directors. The important thing to remember here is that in democratic countries people have the freedom to *act* upon their wishes.

When I visited you, Patricia, we talked about the abundance of phallic symbolism to be found in every part of the world. You were soon to holiday again in Greece, and I wondered if you discovered any 'new' ones there?

Yes, on that occasion we went to Cyprus, and I discovered in the museum at Nicosia, as well as all the usual phallic symbols, a very ancient emblem in one of the cases called the Sacred Cone of Aphrodite. It was about 3½ feet high and was found in the ruins of the temple of Aphrodite at Old Paphos. Apparently, these sacred cones were not uncommon in ancient times, and one from the ruins of Babylon is now in the British Museum.

I bought a book on the history of Cyprus, and it said that King Cinyras of Cyprus founded the original temple of Aphrodite at Old Paphos, along with the custom of religious prostitution, although this was a common practice throughout western Asia and the Middle East, if not elsewhere.

The King's own daughter served the Goddess in this way, and every maiden before marriage was required to give herself to one stranger at the Sanctuary of Aphrodite. This temple was 400 by 230 feet with a court surrounded by porticos, while the shrine itself divided into three separate halls and had a façade surmounted by doves, both living and as carvings. The central hall had a recess which held the original Sacred Cone of the Goddess. What was known as 'The Miraculous Altar of Aphrodite' is said to have stood in the open air quite unprotected, yet was never moistened by rain. The sanctuary was greatly renowned and pictures of it have been found on Greek coins, with gold models of the shrine being discovered in the royal graves at Mycenae.

A story goes that around fifty years ago an archaeologist exploring the temple ruins passed through a farm and in a cow-shed saw some women pouring olive oil on to a cone-shaped white stone. Upon enquiring what they were doing, he was told that it was a very ancient, lucky stone and was anointed in this way by women desiring offspring. He recognized this universal fertility rite and realized that this was the original Sacred Cone. So it appears that the women of Kouklia village near the ruins of Aphrodite's temple continued to anoint Her sacred stone but said that they did it in honour of the Blessed Virgin! The Cone was reproduced on a Roman coin of the first century AD, and was also engraved on gold signet rings. It eventually found its way to the museum in Nicosia.

There was a lovely flower vase in the museum dated around 2500 BC. It was shaped in the form of a phallus and decorated with lines and circles. Vases of this type were used to adorn Aphrodite's altar, and when filled with the scarlet anemones which grow in profusion on Cyprus they must have looked quite beautiful and very effective.

Another mysterious object, upon which early writers have given their various theories, was the Palladium. Some say it was a venerable statue of Pallas Athene; others, that it was a phallic statue of some kind made from the ivory shoulder of Pelops (a character from Greek legend). It was certainly thought to be a priceless possession, as it was kept most secret and the safety of a city is said to have been dependent upon it. Eventually it arrived in Rome where it was hidden in the Penus (food store) of the Temple of Vesta by the Vestal Virgins. They tended the hearth-fire – the focus of the royal line. The Palladium had been passed to them for safe-keeping as a result of the pledge granted by the Fates for the endurance of the royal family's line. If the Palladium *was* a phallic statue of some kind, one wonders what the Vestals thought of it being deposited upon them.

Although these priestesses had to remain chaste for their thirty years of service in the Temple, there may have been times, usually at a midwinter festival such as the Saturnalia, when the rules were slightly relaxed – at least for a special few. It is said that these Vestals were taken at night into a sacred cave and there coupled with high-ranking companions of the royal house, although in the darkness they knew not with whom they lay. If a child was born to a Vestal and became a new king, it was considered to be born of a virgin, or to be the son of a god. This story is supported by the fact that Silvia, the mother of Romulus and Remus, was a Vestal Virgin of Alba Longa (White City), from which Rome was eventually colonized.

Phallic gods were very common in Greece and elsewhere, although they disappeared long ago. One of the most ancient was Mercurius, renamed Hermes by the Greeks. Everywhere there were statues raised in his honour which were termed *Hermae*, and carved in marble with an erect phallus. These were identical to the earlier ones which had venerated Priapus. Often placed in gardens and grottoes, they sometimes had a detachable phallus.

Festivals were held annually in honour of Hermes, notably in Athens, and were similar to those which occurred in Italy when Bacchus was worshipped. The people often carried a *thyrsus* (a cone-tipped wand with two long ribbons attached to it). Of course, the Greeks taught that there was nothing more sacred than physical love, and nothing more beautiful than the nude human body. Echoed in this beauty they said is the song of the nightingale and the blush and perfume of the rose.

I have heard you speak on many occasions, Mrs Crowther, and there is a question I would like to ask you. Why do the priests in your religion wear such ridiculous horned hats?

That you consider the horned helmet to be ridiculous is not at all surprising to me. This is the reaction expected when it is realized that for hundreds of years the Christian Church has taught that anything to do with horns is connected with their Devil and must therefore be regarded as an absurdity, or worse. And this, despite the extravagant headgear their own priests wear, one of which was originally the Ancient Egyptian red and white fish-mouth crown of Upper and Lower Egypt.

In ancient times, the appearance of horns evoked a totally different emotion. They represented power, strength and fertility, and wherever horns were erected this denoted a sacred place or sanctuary. In some areas a huge white crescent, made from white stones, and known as the 'Gate of Horn', was laid down in front of such a shrine. Horns received this kind of approbation when early humans saw that the mightiest and most majestic of animals were thus adorned. And horns even appeared in the night sky – the silver horns of a new moon – surely a symbol of the protection given by the gods.

There are many different cultures in the world whose people continue to wear horns in their rituals and celebrations, and this includes the British Isles. At Abbot's Bromley in Staffordshire there is an annual horned dance which occurs on Wakes Monday, the first Monday after the first Sunday after 4 September. It is performed at the time of the stags' rutting season and is of immeasurable age. The twelve men who perform the dance each wear a pair of reindeer horns. When not in use these are kept in the nearby church of St Nicholas under the vicar's care, and they have been carefully preserved over many centuries. This may seem to be an act of duplicity on the part of Christians, but the people of Abbot's Bromley have never been dissuaded from holding this event, and the Church has, wisely, pulled in its horns!

In Ireland, at Killorglin, Co. Derry, the renowned Puck Fair is celebrated every August. A male goat (the Puck King) is taken from the hills and holds pride of place for the entire festival. He is hoisted on to a platform 35 feet high, festooned with flowers, and regaled with as much food as he can eat. During the three days of the fair, he is crowned with a tinsel crown by a little girl who is named the Queen. On the final day – Scattering Day – the goat is returned safely to *terra firma* and set free again.

The finest example of a pair of horns can be seen at the Palace of Knossos in Crete, where the great carved Horns of Consecration frame the snow-topped peak of Mount Ida, said to enshrine the grave of Zeus. At the time of the astrological Age of Taurus (approximately 4000 to 2000 BC), the bull became the most popular horned animal in many parts of the globe. The Bull Cult of ancient Greece reflected this favoured beast, and again, at Knossos, the dangerous art of bull-leaping was enacted. Daring young men and women diced with death when they grasped a charging bull's horns and somersaulted over its back, to be caught, hopefully, by one of their troupe as they reached the ground. These young acrobats were drawn from different parts of Greece, particularly Athens, and must have been very highly trained in such a precarious activity. Even so, deaths were recorded, and families must have prayed for the safety of a son or daughter.

It should be remembered that, despite the negativity given to horns by the Christians, the Bible speaks of them in a positive manner, and in phrases such as, 'The horns of the righteous shall be exalted', 'Mine horn is exalted in the Lord' and, most notably, 'The horns of the altar'.

The horn, as a powerful, thrusting, masculine symbol, becomes a feminine object when inverted and used as a cup or container. The cornucopia or 'Horn of Plenty', filled with fruit and flowers, has long been considered as a token of good luck and protection. Its origins come from the Greek legend of Zeus who was suckled on the milk of a goat. In one of the various versions of this story, his nurse, a nymph named Amalthea, was rewarded by the God when he broke off one of the goat's horns and endowed it with marvellous properties including the power of becoming filled with whatever the possessor might wish for. This, he presented to Amalthea. The goat, he placed in the stars.

The protective quality of horns can be seen in the ancient hand-sign of the *mano cornuta* or 'making horns' where the first and little fingers of the hand are held up while the other two are held down by the thumb. This is used to ward off the 'evil eye' or other negative influences.

So, the horned helmet worn by the High Priest of a coven, when correctly understood, is merely upholding a tradition which can be equated with the wearing of a crown: both are echoing ancient values of power and nobility, and by the process of symbiosis automatically transform the wearer into a magically-empowered human being.

What was the difference between the rural fertility cults and the urban mystery cults of the ancient world?

There was certainly a difference between them, even in approach to their gods. However, despite this disparity, both cults would have worshipped the gods indigenous to their culture and race.

Rural cults were more interested in the fertility of the land than of people. Their rites would be conducted outdoors, in woods or in isolated places. Not for them the adornments of ritualistic dress or of performing their rites in beautiful marble temples. These things personified wealth which they did not possess. What they *did* possess, however, was nature, in abundance. Being amidst the Great Mother's bounty and feeling her presence all around them must have given a feeling of exhilaration and joy. There could be no better place in which to adore their gods and work magic.

Ancient stone altars bear witness to what they believed – a single, solitary standing stone, pointing to the heavens, was often all they needed to focus upon in their magical practices. Their rites, too, would differ to some extent from those in cities or other populated areas. And not only differ, but would be known only by those who participated in them.

The great temples of the ancient world were each dedicated to different deities and, apart from the main altar to whom the temple was built, there would be separate rooms which contained altars to other well-known gods. These temples were huge constructions, beautifully wrought, which often lasted far into the new Christian era, but were eventually destroyed, or left to fall into disrepair, their stones used for building purposes. One such site was the Sanctuary at Eleusis, not far from Athens. This sanctuary was the centre of a religious cult which existed for nearly two thousand years and whose initiates came from all parts of the civilized world.

The first religious building was erected on the mountain slope at Eleusis in the fifteenth century BC. It is known to archaeologists as 'Megaron B' and through its various transformations it was identified as a building for use in a mystic cult. The expanse of the completed area consisted of a temple to Demeter, the Great Hall, the Telesterion – 'filled with pillars and rows of seating were only a part of "this huge site" ' where both the Greater and the Lesser Mysteries of the Goddess were enacted. What can safely be called the highest and most noble initiatory process in Greece took place at Eleusis. And it cannot be disputed that the different stages of these mysteries gave the initiates theoretical knowledge which transformed their view of the cosmos and their place within it.

The Lesser Mysteries were taught collectively to large numbers of people, while the Greater Mysteries were conducted individually and contained within them the act of passing symbolically through the 'Gates of Death'. Some secrets at Eleusis, such as the 'password to the Paradise of Demeter' to be employed after death, were given by word of mouth. Demeter's symbols of corn, pomegranates and poppies, carved on the stone pillars and entrances, together with the presentation of an ear of corn at the end of the sacred drama, all pointed to the presence of unseen forces which affected not only the vegetable kingdom, but equally the life of humans.

For onlookers, there must have been some wondrous happening – a collective vision which left a lasting sense of awe and an unforgettable memory of the drama. The goddess, Demeter, her daughter, Persephone, and the Mysteries at Eleusis, were undoubtedly the apex of spiritual knowledge and the most important aspect of pagan thought and religion in Ancient Greece. The mere fact of the Mysteries being kept secret for at least fifteen hundred years speaks of the sacredness in which they were held. Plutarch, an initiate of the Greater Mysteries, said that when death comes it is like initiation, and Apuleius, before his initiation, was told that it was similar to a voluntary death followed by a slow recovery.

It can therefore be seen that the differences between cults in the ancient world were many and varied, yet anchored together by their sacred pantheon of gods, in which the Great Goddess, in any of Her guises, was paramount.

If you can, go to Eleusis and sit by Demeter's sacred well. Offer a libation of wine, and be filled with a sense of wonder at this place still called the Sanctuary at Eleusis.

Can a person truly connect with the God and the Goddess if they do not belong to the Craft?

Yes, of course they can! There are thousands of neo-pagans around today who also know and believe in the Old Gods. However, not all souls are ready to take initiation through the Craft, as this entails a life-long commitment. Unless a person feels deeply within that they must begin that Journey and become a Child of the Goddess, it is far better that they pursue the Path of the Pagan, or whatever path feels right for them. They may not practise the rites of the Craft, or know the Divine Pair as their spiritual guides, but as the universal twin forces of life itself, the God and Goddess can be recognized and revered by anyone.

12 Symbols and Spells

We live in a world filled with symbols of every kind. In some cases they are made as a type of shorthand which we can immediately link to external objects without the use of sentences to explain them. Magical symbols, however, are mostly extremely ancient, and like magical alphabets were constructed on Inner as well as Outer levels of consciousness. When used correctly, magical symbols connect the conscious mind with Inner Intelligences. Such forces or Beings are adept at understanding what is meant by a particular symbol, and therefore are able to give whatever spiritual aid is required. Nevertheless, the operator should be fully cognisant with the symbol they are using. A thorough study is needed in order to learn a symbol's exact meaning on both outer and inner levels. It is this ability to examine the spiritual 'interior' of a symbol and know its 'message' that generates the necessary magical power when used in the Art.

Magical alphabets were often composed of pictures or sigils and were also used for spells, appropriate signs or figures being incorporated into the words – or spelling it out. Doreen Valiente and I created a secret magical alphabet which we utilized when exchanging letters – a very useful tool when writing on magical matters in case letters went astray.

*Many witches use shells and fossils in their spells, and sometimes deco-
rate their altars with them. Do you think these things are magical?*

When I hold a fossil in my hand and consider that millions of
years ago it was a living creature, I certainly find it wondrous,
and yes, magical. You might say that the whole of nature is magical. Just to think that nature has changed what was once a living
thing to stone is quite remarkable. Fossils have long been considered to be mysterious for this reason, and witches prefer an
uncommon artefact to an everyday one. Another important
reason for using fossils is that like horn or ivory they once had
life in them.

It is thought to be very lucky to find an ammonite on the
beach. I have found several during the years I have spent at my
cottage in Whitby. The coiled shape of the stone is symbolic of the
spiral of life and of evolution, and has always been regarded with
a certain reverence. Three ammonites compose the crest of
Whitby itself, and of course there are silly legends about them
made up by the Christians, as with most ancient things. No
doubt superstitious folk in the olden days believed these stories,
as ammonites abound in this area.

The 'Shepherd's Crown' is a lovely type of fossil having a
heart shape with a five-pointed star pattern on the top. It is cred-
ited with great magical properties. Another variety, but more
rounded, is called 'Fairy Loaves' and its magical associations are
many and varied. These are fossilized sea-urchins and have been
discovered as grave goods in neolithic burials, and more recently
were placed upon windowsills to avert the 'Evil Eye' and to
protect the house from lightning and witchcraft. If a ploughman
found one he would spit on it, throw it three times in the air, then
over his left shoulder, for luck.

Another interesting fossil is the Belemnite, sometimes known
as a 'thunder stone' or 'thunder bolt'. Belemnites are actually the
inner shell of a cephalopod, or Savid-type fish, similar to the
squid. Its phallic shape, long and pointed, made it doubly magical. Barren women used to wear one close to the skin, and they

were often carried as luck-bringers.

Most noteworthy among fossils must be the *Porosphaera globularis* or 'witch stone'. Any stone with a hole through it is said to be very lucky, but the real witch stone is not stone at all. It is a fossilized sponge, again millions of years old, and small, round, white and faintly glittering – really beautiful. It is also perforated through the centre. In Whitby Museum there is a necklace of them labelled, 'The Oldest Necklace in the World', a true statement. Always thought of as extremely powerful and magical, they were worn as necklaces and a ponderous string of them would be hung behind the door of a home to ward off evil. Their shape immediately links them with the female and, therefore, the Mother Goddess, which enhanced their beneficial reputation even more. I found enough of them on Brighton beach to make a necklace, along with a little heart-shaped stone for the thread to go over as a fastener. It is consecrated and only worn in the Circle.

There are literally thousands of different kinds of shells in the world. These are mostly the abandoned homes of sea creatures and occur in a wide variety of shapes. Shells are most beautifully constructed and really are one of nature's miracles. They differ enormously in size, from the very small, to the huge, pink-mouthed ones which need two hands to hold them. Among their different patterns are the conical or pointed, and the round or hollow, which have naturally been recognized as male and female symbols. Anything which suggested the twin forces of life was regarded as holy and, in that sense, the bringers of luck and protection. I have a large 'female' shell in my bathroom, and one day attempted to dust it, only to find it had become the home of a spider who was most indignant about the intrusion, so I desisted from cleaning it forthwith!

In Greek and Roman art the shell most frequently depicted was the scallop. Botticelli's famous painting 'The Birth of Venus' shows the goddess standing in a scallop shell. A beautiful earthenware vase in the Hermitage Museum at Leningrad has the same goddess rising from between the valves of a scallop. She is graced with pearls and has a garland in her hair. The vase was found at Taman, near the Black Sea, and is dated to around 400 BC. The sacredness of shells is shown by the reverence in which they were used. The grave-stone memorial of a high priestess of the Mother Goddess, now in the Vatican Museum, portrays the priestess backed by a huge scallop shell which gives her the necessary dignity which she no doubt had in life. In Christian art-forms, too, the Virgin Mary is often surrounded by shells, and in Pontevedra in Spain, the little church was designed in the form of a scallop shell.

Mrs Crowther, how do you think the various magical symbols of the Craft came into being?

I suspect, in a variety of ways. In very ancient times, people saw pictures and symbols in all kinds of natural phenomena. I say in ancient times, because there are not many people today who bother to look around them and/or contemplate the views in the countryside – or even their own gardens. Certainly, the face of what we now call the 'Green Man' was first seen in the foliage of a tree.

Symbols such as a triangle or a pentagram were easily observed by seeing a naked woman. Her pubic area is in the form of a triangle; and if a man or a woman stand with their legs apart and their arms raised from their sides, this makes a very good outline of a pentagram or five-pointed star. These symbols were very naturally incorporated into the ancient magical operations, and early representations of the Goddess always emphasized the Triangle by incising that part of a statue in deep lines. It became known most appropriately as the 'Triangle of Water' and was often painted blue; it thus repre-sented the Waters of Life and the Waters of the Womb through which life is engendered. Water flows downwards, but the flames of fire dart upwards, so an upward-pointing triangle sometimes coloured red became a symbol for that element. These two triangles, interlaced, became known as the

160

'hexagram' or, when used by the Hebrews, the 'Star of David'. (Curiously, an old German name for a witch was *hexe*.) This most magical and ancient symbol denotes the marriage of Water (female) and Fire (male), which can be interpreted on many levels.

The five-pointed star, or pentagram, has long been associated with witchcraft and with magic generally, the points representing the four elements plus the spirit. It is also called the 'Endless Knot', as it can be drawn with one stroke of the pen.

The Crowned Pentagram however, is peculiar to the Craft of the Wise and is a symbol of its Priesthood. This pentagram has an upward-pointing triangle above it, the whole being emblematic of the spiritual objective of the Craft. The Triangle reveals the Godhead or Absolute at the top, from which issues the male and female forces of life, intimated by the two remaining points. The Crowned Pentagram has thirteen sides which equate with the thirteen full moons in a year and the number of a full coven. The symbol has eight points, representing the sacred number of the Craft, and the figure 8 is seen as symbolizing two worlds touching – the physical and the spiritual. Eight is also echoed in the number of magical tools, the paths towards illumination, and the Eight Ritual Occasions or festivals of the year. A reversed pentagram becomes the face of the Horned God in certain dramatic rituals.

There is yet further fascinating information concerning the great age of the pentagram which I discovered in the book *Uriel's Machine*, by Christopher Knight and Robert Lomas. The work has many facets and reveals how science began in Western Europe over five thousand years ago. It shows that important megalithic sites in the British Isles were engineered to measure the long-term movements of the planet Venus, and provided a time-keeping system accurate to a few seconds over a forty-year period. This forty-year period is calculated from the time of a superior conjunction with the sun and the planet's first appearance in the evening sky.

Every eight years, Venus marks a point when the solar calendar, the lunar calendar and the sidereal calendar all coincide to within a few minutes. Over five Venus Cycles – every forty years – it synchronizes these calendars to within a few seconds. But these five Venus Cycles also make a remarkable pattern in the sky and around the circle of the Zodiac: that of a perfect pentagram or a five-pointed star. There, in the heavens, is the symbol of the Craft created by Venus – a shining reflection of the Goddess Herself.

So, in these stellar movements, which were known over five thousand years ago, we have: eight, the number of the Craft; forty, which has always been a sacred number in the Mysteries; five, the points of a pentagram; and in the starry heavens, the five-pointed star itself, produced by Venus – the ancient Goddess of Love! I think that we should consider that the origins of the Craft, and the symbols within it, could indeed be more ancient than we have hitherto imagined.

Patricia, I have heard about something called a 'Witch's Ladder'. Do you know what it is?

The Witch's Ladder is a length of cord or rope with nine knots tied along it and evenly spaced out. In each knot there is a feather. All the feathers are in different colours, and they come from nine different birds. The knots represent the spells cast, and the feathers symbolize those for whom the spells are worked. The Witch's Ladder is mostly used when a group of people, or a family, require the same or similar magical results for themselves, and for an identical reason. Today, the Witch's Ladder is generally used to improve the health and happiness of a household, or people who live together or near to each other. In ancient times however, it could quite easily have been employed to banish or rid the witches of troublesome neighbours, or those who were in league with the witch-finders themselves. In these cases only black feathers were used, taken from a crow or a raven.

Are curses for real, Mrs Crowther? If so, how do you rid yourself of one?

A curse is a very real attack upon a person's subconscious mind, either by thought or by the spoken word. If the latter, it will naturally startle the one receiving it and, if the person is already a timid soul, will have a greater effect than upon a stronger personality.

It has been discovered that the active 'receiving and thinking' part of the mind reacts upon the subconscious – the innermost storehouse of hidden emotions, fears and impressions which governs our reactions in everyday matters. A curse transferred by pure thought manifests as a heaviness – an uncertain feeling that all is not well. This feeling is a warning given by the higher self. Occultists have their own methods of dealing with such horrid things, which usually results in the curse being returned very swiftly to its originator. But for those without esoteric interests, the best thing to do is as follows. Every morning and evening (until you feel a positive change has occurred), look at yourself in a mirror, and concentrate very hard upon being in control of your own mind and body, and of being master of your destiny. Make up a short verse to this effect, such as: 'My life is my own, and henceforth will be transformed and improved!' Say it aloud to your reflection at least three times. By this method you are reconditioning your subconscious mind and breaking the curse.

A mirror can also be used to deflect hostile thoughts by turning it to face the direction you believe the psychic attack is coming from or, if you don't know, showing it to the four points of the compass, saying: 'Return from whence thou came. I repudiate thee! Begone! Begone! Begone!' Or make up your own sentence on the same lines. And not only pronounce the words, but summon up your determination and strength to banish this assault upon you. The success of any magical ritual depends upon the energy that is put into it.

Mirrors have been used in magic for a variety of reasons. In

Ancient Egypt the Mirror of Hathor, a polished, oval, bronze mirror on a long thin handle, carved in the form of the Goddess, was regarded as being an extremely potent adjunct to the working of magic. It also functioned as a special instrument for scrying, being sacred to the Goddess Herself. And yet another of this mirror's powers was that it could deflect any evil thoughts back upon an assailant. No doubt a particular prayer to Hathor was uttered when it was used in this way, as one of her aspects is comparable to the Greek goddess Athene, in that she only fights in order to defend.

Patricia, can witches raise the wind?

It is generally accepted that witches can raise winds. The reason for this is because the element of Air is more malleable than the other three, Earth, Water and Fire. Also, Air links easily with the mind and with the whole of our bodies, as we inhale and exhale it constantly. Another reason is that human beings exist upon a higher level than the elements, so it follows that those who know the secrets of magic are in a position to control or alter the winds, if the need arises. Winds, of course, bring clouds, and clouds usually bring rain. Winds also raise storms at sea, so you can begin to understand the different effects which can be gained through raising this element.

It is certain that in order to deter the Spanish Armada, witches and other occultists raised great winds which caused huge storms at sea, the like of which had never before been observed. And this was also done during the reign of Napoleon, for the same reasons.

In olden days wise women would often sell winds to sailors on the eve of a voyage. This was done by means of a cord which had at least three knots in it. If a sailor required a light breeze to spring up, he would unfasten a knot. When a wind was needed he would untie a further knot, and for a really strong wind to arise, he would unfasten yet another knot. And seagoing men swore that this magic worked. I also believe that it worked, as the

164

method was used so often and was known to bring the required results over a long period of time. Belief in magic is obviously one of the reasons why it works, but there is also an unknown 'something' – an esoteric mystery – which lies behind all human effort and which even practitioners of magic comprehend yet do not wholly understand. One might call it Fate, or the name by which it was known in olden days – the Ancient Providence.

13 Miscellaneous Questions and Answers

In The Old Sod, the life of William G. Gray *by Alan Richardson and Marcus Claridge, the authors infer that Gray influenced the Craft and that, until his* Seasonal Occult Rituals *was published in 1970, many new witches never linked their rites with the seasons. Is this true?*

Let's put it this way. I have never known a witch who was ignorant of the fact that the entire system of the Craft is based upon: the Wheel of the Year; the signs of the Zodiac; the Four Seasons; and, most importantly, the Four Cross-Quarter days, i.e. Beltane, Lammas, Samhain and Imbolc. The latter are the four oldest festivals of the nature year and are based in the centre of the four fixed signs of the Zodiac. The Equinoxes and Solstices make up the other four festivals, for what is known in the Craft as the Eight Ritual Occasions. So I think the answer to that part of the question is, 'No!'

Bill was a great friend of mine and a very clever magician. He was also a Qabalist, a discipline which is based on the Hermetic Path, whereas most Pagan traditions are based upon the Orphic Path. The famous 'Tree of Life' diagram displays both these Paths, and they both lead to illumination. To put it plainly, it is just a matter of deciding which one suits you, and whether you

166

are principally a *thinking* or a *feeling* individual.

Although Bill's opinion of witchcraft was, to put it mildly, extremely low, he noticed how popular the Craft was becoming, and how many hundreds of souls who had been bereft of the Feminine Principle in Divinity, known as the Great Goddess, were being drawn towards this most important and necessary part of their existence. There was also the wild, pagan aspect of the Old Religion, where freedom in worship could be experienced by dancing sky-clad in the glades and being 'at one' with nature. It was all a far cry from sitting in the cold tombs of churches listening to the droning voice of the minister uttering his monotonous and boring admonitions. So, as early as 1968, Bill took the cue and easily wrote his *Seasonal Occult Rituals*. I say easily, because his knowledge more than encompassed the four elements, their qualities and their spirit, which are an essential part of these rituals.

The difficulty came when the manuscript had been written and required a publisher. Apparently, either the wrong publishers were contacted, or they did not believe that such a book would be successful. This is often the way with publishers, who are very cautious people. Therefore, Bill asked Bobbie (his wife), Arnold and me if we would work some magic for his manuscript, and one evening we all piled into our car and set off for the Rollright Stones. During the week we were staying with Bill and Bobbie we repeated the ritual again at the Rollright Circle, and on both occasions the nights were fine and clear and without interruptions, apart from a passenger in one car being driven past who popped his head out of the window and yelled, 'Lovely night for the witches, then?'

Our work seemed to have been successful when, a few weeks later, Bill wrote to say that his manuscript had been accepted for publication. Truth to tell, I had never seen Bill so worried and so anxious about a manuscript. Bobbie would say, 'Oh God, he's on about that b——y book, again, we'll have to do some more work for him, to keep him quiet!' However, all came right in the end and Bobbie was once more able to do her own work in peace.

Do I think that Bill influenced the Craft? No, I don't, and in light of his *Seasonal Occult Rituals* I would say rather the reverse. But he told me many interesting and magical things which made a lot of sense. And I think he discovered that not all witches were brainless idiots, as he supposed. He often remarked that the best people he worked with were all witches, and coming from Bill this was surely a compliment. I certainly enjoyed working with such experienced occultists as Bill and Bobbie. It broadened my own knowledge of magic and was so refreshing. It was also a change for the *mind* – a change from purely Craft rituals, however inestimable they may be. Change is very important to me, and they do say it is as good as a rest. It invigorates my mind so that, later, I can return to my original work with new enthusiasm. Bill Gray also had many changes in his life, which I believe all culminated in making him a fount of knowledge and a true master Magician.

Pat, why is the left hand associated with the Devil?

In the past, it was certainly associated with evil, hence the word 'sinistro' or 'sinister' which comes from the Latin for the left side. It was thought that all witches were left-handed, as it was taught that all witches were evil. We have the Christian Church to thank for this rubbish, which they fed to their congregations on every possible occasion. Some witches *were* left-handed but there is a valid reason for this; it is, if you like, one of the secrets of the Craft.

For these reasons, up to the 1930s, and possibly later, school-children were strictly forbidden to write with the left hand and, if they showed a predilection for using that hand, it was tied behind their backs until they had learned their lesson. It is hardly believable that such execrable things actually crept into education. Everything was linked with black or white, left or right, positive or negative, but just because something is negative does not mean that it is evil. The preference for writing with the left or the right hand reveals whether a child will become mostly a feeling or a thinking individual. If a child is ambidextrous – can write with both hands and equally well – this usually portends an advanced soul who will become a shining light in life.

This impulse for writing with one hand or the other stems from the fact that the brain is divided into two hemispheres. The left side connects with the practical, the mathematical and good old commonsense, while the right side stresses the poetic, artistic and mystical. Emphasis from the *right* hemisphere promotes use of the *left* hand and vice versa.

While I am writing upon the subject of the brain, it should be realized that the source of clairvoyance appears to stem from the pineal gland. This gland is situated centrally in the brain and aligned between the eyes. It is known as the 'Third Eye' and has been recognized in many cultures. The ancient Egyptians represented this Third Eye upon their statuary by placing an eye in the middle of the forehead between the physical eyes.

When clairvoyance occurs, the vision beams out from the forehead a little above the physical eyes, at least it did for me when I first experienced it during a meeting when we were working for someone. It was truly amazing, as on that first occasion I was looking at a scene in astral colours a little way in front of my face. I later learned that was connected with the person for whom we were working magic, but I did not know it at the time. That this ability is part of the human condition is still a wonder to me. And the fact that the rites of the Craft can induce it, is again proof of their veracity and importance. What I 'saw' that night was something which had happened to the person *in the previous year*. The pineal gland has the ability to portray past, present and future, but its function has been deliberately forgotten by those who did not want people to know that they possessed a sixth sense. Consequently, for a long time, clairvoyants were very secretive, but were single-minded enough to develop the art for themselves. Certainly, it was always practised within the Craft and was vital in times of danger.

You have mentioned the Four Tides and how they operate in your book
Lid off the Cauldron, *Patricia, but could you explain their origins –*
where they emanate from?

The Four Tides cover the entire Northern Hemisphere irrespective of climate. In the Southern Hemisphere the Tides are the
same but the opposite way round – our winter is their summer,
our autumn is their spring, etc. Although parts of America are
virtually seasonless, they are still part of the Northern
Hemisphere. The witches who live there observe the nature year
in accordance with the rest of the Northern Hemisphere, celebrating the Eight Festivals at the same times as the rest of us. The
fact that they have no seasons as such does not seem to worry
them – nor should it.

Although the Four Tides have an effect upon the physical
plane, they originate upon the Astral Plane and flow freely in the
astral light. This is the environment of most magical operations
which focus on the Lunar sphere. And it is upon the Astral Plane
that successful lunar magic is wrought. So you will understand
why it is important to recognize the nature and constancy of
these seasonal tides, not least because of their vital influence in
connection with the workings of this type of magic.

The Four Tides result from two consequences – the major one
being the effect of solar particles which bombard the Earth's
odic mantle, and the secondary one concerning the stresses
occurring within the odic mantle by reason of the Earth's axial
inclination.

As you say, I have written about the Four Tides elsewhere, but
I would like to stress that the 'Tide of Purification' – from the
Winter Solstice to the Vernal Equinox – has always been known by
occultists as the *Tempus Eversionis*. It should be regarded as a time
of *withdrawal*, excellent for meditation, visualizations, prayer and
purification of oneself. It is a time for cleansing the working area
and getting rid of unwanted clutter, outworn habits, and so on. It
is nonetheless a *positive* Tide and so powerful that to perform any
magical work within it would be tantamount to asking the heav-

ens to fall upon your head. Trends set in motion in this Tide have
been known to become revitalized in the Tide of Activation in a
negative and distorted fashion creating a chaotic effect. Although
this tide is positive, the energy – the Power of Growth – is withheld
from the Earth in this Tide. It is slowly released *after* the Vernal
Equinox when life begins again.

There are yet other Tides (but not so strong as the Four Tides)
which are considered by occultists and witches in their work.
These flow from East to West and are known as the 'Tattvic
Tides'. They align with the hours of the day and the night. A list
of them is included in the appendix of my *Lid off the Cauldron* and
in various other works on the subject of Magic.

Is there any pagan symbolism in the architecture around Sheffield?

There are two statues in the city centre. We have a large figure of
the smith god Vulcan on the top of our Town Hall, a most suitable god for a city which is renowned for its manufacture of steel.
And there is a statue of Mercury crowning the Sheffield newspaper buildings. Mercury is the Messenger of the Gods who,
among his many attributes, governs the spoken and written
word.

I found the carving of a male head on the side of a wall in the
city centre, high up, above an old narrow lane. It is a fine carving
of a bearded face surrounded by foliage.

A friend of mine discovered two stone heads on buildings in a
residential area: one, of a beautiful lady framed with flowers; the
other, a splendid portrayal of the Green Man.

So many lovely old buildings in Sheffield have been demol-
ished in order to make way for concrete monstrosities – office
blocks, etc., and no doubt the same thing occurs elsewhere. I am
sure that much ornamental stonework was lost in the process. J.
Edward Vickers, the late Sheffield historian, and his friends,
managed to save some buildings from being destroyed, including
the Lyceum Theatre, which thankfully is still thriving. But I do
think it would be a good idea for people to look around their own

local areas for interesting symbols, especially pagan ones, and record them in their own archives for posterity. You never know what you may find by programming yourself for this kind of discovery. A very worthwhile one, too.

I know you do much work for animals in distress, Pat. Can you tell us a little about this side of your work?

There are so many instances of animal cruelty throughout the world, but unfortunately there is only so much that we can do to negate these obscenities. Often, we work to help a domesticated animal in trouble. A dog called Sam lived in Sheffield with his master, who was a warden at a home for the aged. The old ladies loved him and he would keep them company for hours on end. Then suddenly, someone on the Sheffield Council decided that Sam could not stay at the home, and he was banished to kennels. I rang Sam's master and he was very upset about it, but was frightened of losing his employment if he protested. So we worked a magical rite for Sam, and waited. One evening Ian, my partner, was perusing the local newspaper and suddenly called out, 'Sam Stays'. The penny did not drop immediately, so I asked 'What did you say?' Ian, infuriatingly, merely repeated, 'Sam Stays', so I looked over his shoulder and saw that he was reading the headline of an article about Sam. Yes, he was back with his ladies and loving every minute of being fussed over. There was a lovely picture of Sam, with his ladies, too. Apparently, the councillor had a change of heart.

Do you remember the Sigil we made for the animals back in the 1990s, Patricia? I wonder if it is still being used?

When my friend, Christina, who lives in Vienna, asked me this question, I thought it would be an excellent idea for the Sigil to be introduced again in this book. It first appeared in the American occult magazine, *The Hidden Path*, but it is such a beautiful work of art that it deserves to be recognized and magically empowered by all witches and occultists who love and care for animals and birds. Here is the original text by Christina Koehldorfer and Peter Stockinger, explaining its construction and significance.

> The Sigil is simple to draw and easy to keep in mind, which is very important. It encompasses *five* symbols. Each one stands for an entire group of animals, and one symbol represents all birds (see illustration).
>
> The SIGIL must be empowered by you, in your own particular way, so that its effect infiltrates the mind of a person, who has – consciously or unconsciously – seen it. Ergo, every man, woman and child who notices this SIGIL will begin to realize the cruelty and torture that is often meted out to the Animal and Bird Kingdom with whom we share this planet, and thus be made aware of it. Please help us to make the SIGIL strong! The stronger it becomes, the better for the animals and the birds. Circulate it as far as possible. Copy it and place it wherever you can. For example, upon your garden gate; in a window; and in a window of your car. A copy was passed to a close friend and she too is spreading the SIGIL the same way. This friend does *not* know about the magical power of the SIGIL, but she too is circulating it because she also loves the wildlife. Telling her that circulating this symbol will help the animals was enough; she did not ask for further information. People have to *see* the SIGIL so that it can begin to change their minds.
>
> Thanks to all of you who will help the animals and the birds by working on this project. Thank you! May the Goddess and Her Consort be with you. Blessed Be.

The sigil is so harmonious and evocative, that I dare to suggest it came from realms other than the physical. But for it to be a perpetual sigil of magical force, it must be regularly and repeatedly charged, with words such as, 'Compassion for the animals and birds', or 'Respect and care for the animals and birds', while concentrating upon people treating them well.

 SYMBOL FOR ALL ANIMALS WITH PAWS

 SYMBOL FOR ALL BIRDS

 SYMBOL FOR ALL HOOFED ANIMALS

 SYMBOL FOR ALL REPTILES

 SYMBOL FOR ALL ANIMALS LIVING IN THE WATERS

 THE PROTECTION WE GIVE TO THE ANIMALS

What is the Shadow Self, and how do I learn about it?

The Shadow Self is another term for the Inner Self. Most occultists know about this 'other self' through their studies and magical operations. The Godhead divides at some point into male and female polarities in order to bring everything into existence; at least, that is how the miracle of life is viewed, and no doubt operates. And these male and female polarities are recognized as the God and Goddess – the great forces of Life, itself. These opposites exist everywhere in nature, and are copied in the physical bodies of men and women. They are called the *animus* and the *anima* (male and female). The entire universe was erected upon the fusion of these two principles and, right down to the smallest cell, this process would seem to be enacted and re-enacted, *ad infinitum*.

In the study and practice of magic, it is known that the poles are reversed; the female becomes the positive pole and the male becomes the negative pole. And this reversal connects intimately with the Inner or Shadow Self, which is of the opposite sex to the flesh. This is one of the great secrets of magic. The act of performing a magical rite is actually that of imitating the actions of the Godhead, of putting oneself in the position of the Godhead, in order to change an existing situation or problem by mental prowess.

To become adept in the Magical Arts, it is necessary to develop and be in rapport with your Inner Self, so that when performing magic the twin selves – the Physical Self and the Shadow Self – are working together and echoing the Godhead. The female therefore, becomes the Positive Pole in magic, and is the chief sources of Magical Power, which is one of the reasons why a woman has the superior position in witchcraft. The male, being the Negative Pole in the Circle, supports the female, and does the work of forming and energizing the mental image created by the female on Astral levels.

The ritual of Cakes and Wine in the Craft reveals this ancient knowledge. The female holds the *masculine* symbol of the athame, while the male holds the *feminine* symbol of the cup.

Thus revealing the reversal of the Poles.

Realization of the Inner Self is therefore a prerequisite in magic, and this must be accompanied by its cultivation. Learn to know it and love it – after all it is part of *you*. Scrying may also help you to gain a closer relationship with your Shadow Self. It will help if you were born with a harmonious blending of male and female aspects in your natal astrological chart. Are the planets distributed evenly in masculine and feminine signs, or is there a predominance of one or the other? Correcting a slight imbalance can be achieved by meditating upon a masculine or feminine tool of the Craft (whichever is pertinent) and by using them regularly in private.

Patricia, could you please give your views on the afterlife, as understood in the Craft. I have read about your psychic experiences in your books, but don't know what really happens after the death of the body.

Witches are taught that after death their souls enter what is known in the Craft as the Summerland. This is only a vague allusion to after-death experiences, and it did not satisfy me. In the Old Religion we believe in reincarnation but, again, nothing is explained in detail. From the viewpoint of practising the rituals, methods of releasing the spirit and of gaining an altered state of consciousness, nothing is lacking since these methods are excellent and have been proved so, times without number. There are also ways for discovering aspects of previous lives, and for learning about the Higher Self, which again have been tried and tested over a long period of time. But, as I say, I wanted to know more of the spiritual planes, so I read widely on the subject, including the works of famous occult teachers from different parts of the world.

What I found out made perfect sense and harmonized with my own psychic experiences. I discussed what I had learned on the subject in my autobiography, and also in *The Zodiac Experience*. I think it is wonderful to learn that the Inner Planes are linked with natural phenomena; that they are each composed of the ethereal qualities of an element – Water, Air or Fire; and that they are positioned in that order of sequence and refinement from the Earth Plane. In other words, the Inner Planes (or as much as we know of them) are a reflection of these three elements in their finer, more subtle states. After the death of the body, most souls enter the Astral Plane which, being composed of the inner dimensions of Water, is fluidic and malleable.

The Silver Cord having been severed, the soul slips into this Plane in its Astral Body. If the soul is of greater refinement than astral conditions, it will be drawn into a finer dimension or State of Being. Witches and occultists realize that we have *three* bodies: the physical, the etheric and the astral. The etheric body is closely linked to the physical body and, after death, its vibrations return to the World of Matter. The astral body, however, is that of the *emotions*, and therefore a fitting vehicle for containment (however temporary) of the soul or spirit.

It is said that there are many different divisions or levels of the Astral Plane. The Lower Astral contains the spirits of animals and birds, including those beloved pets who will automatically be drawn to those who loved them in life. Love is the Key, which surmounts all boundaries, and it is the *raison d'être* for Life itself.

Finer than the Astral Plane is the Manasic Plane, which aligns with the inner dimensions of Air. You will notice that this Plane also has a proper *name* by which it is known, mainly in the East. Manasic or *mens*, meaning the Mind. This is the Plane of pure bliss, which is known variously as Heaven, Nirvana, the Summerlands, etc. Here, the soul exists as pure thought in light. When one sees a vision of a loved one who has passed on, clothed in light, *that* soul has attained the Manasic Plane, its astral body having been left behind to dissolve on astral levels.

Beyond the Manasic Plane lies the Plane of Masterhood, or Godhood. This links with the spiritual dimensions of Fire and, therefore, Light. It is said that this Plane is beyond the comprehension of most mortals, but there dwell the great spirits, teachers and avatars who have conquered karma, and who may voluntarily reincarnate to teach a new influence in the ever-changing ages of the world. Doubtless, there are yet other Planes of existence of which humanity as yet knows nothing but, which, at the appropriate time in our evolutionary progress will be revealed.

I feel strongly about this subject because at many of my lectures to groups representing diverse stratas of society, there is always an interest in life after death from people who tell me they know nothing about it. When I refer to the different Planes of existence, they ask, 'But where are these Planes?' to which I reply, 'Well, you cannot see the air that you breathe, and yet it is a very dense gas. Just because you cannot see a thing, does not prevent it from being a reality.'

This subject has been ignored for too long: either through ignorance or disinterest. People have been kept in the dark for hundreds of years, principally in the West, by Christianity, and now, at the beginning of the Age of Aquarius, it is high time that they became more enlightened. Today, religious beliefs are largely ignored by those who have no specific interest in spiritual matters, but for people who *are* interested and willing to listen, witches and pagans should give them some idea at least of after-life conditions. Even speaking to someone on a one-to-one basis, you will be increasing awareness, giving encouragement, and fulfilling the occult law, 'I wish to learn in order to serve'.

What lessons have you learned from acting, Patricia, that are useful for a High Priestess?

Many! I was trained in dancing, deportment, voice production, drama and music (accordion and piano), and most of these areas have been useful in my occult work, not to mention earning a living in the theatre. It should be understood that all ritual involves *acting*. You are acting out a part. The voice, therefore, is very important; in fact your whole being enters into the ritual and the words that you are declaiming. Any ritual will fail if the words of a rite are mumbled or merely read from the book, or if a High Priestess or High Priest is unable to perform their role effectively. However, the process of learning and of involvement in the Craft casts its own magic, and I have found that those who become leaders are also magically transformed through the God and the Goddess, and function with more magnetism and proficiency than could have been imagined at their initiations. It really is quite amazing and quite wonderful.

I have heard that ouija boards can be used to contact spirits. What exactly are they, and do witches use them?

The ouija board, covered with letters and numbers, was invented, as you say, to communicate with souls who have passed to the spirit world. 'Oui-ja' is French and German respectively for 'yes'. A guided glass is allowed to spell out words or sentences from the board, which it is hoped will provide useful information from beyond the grave.

Another implement, which is also an aid to automatic writing, is the planchette. This takes the form of a heart-shaped wooden board, about the size of a human hand, with small wheels and fitted with a pen or pencil pointing downwards. The planchette is guided by the user's hand resting gently upon it, and what is written on the paper underneath is considered to be the thoughts of a departed soul.

The operator must clear their mind of any extraneous thoughts and allow themselves to become a channel for this type of spirit communication. Of course, mediums can do the same thing by holding a writing implement above a sheet of paper. I once received a message in this manner, which I have related elsewhere.

I have never heard of witches using ouija boards, although some may do so. Any communication from the spiritual realms usually comes orally through the High Priestess, or another witch in the Circle, and sometimes quite unexpectedly. Messages of this nature are always recorded in order to check their veracity and to preserve them.

The ouija board is mostly used by spiritualists and those who are constantly requested by the bereaved to be put in touch with loved ones, although most mediums are able to transmit messages solely through their gifts of clairvoyance or clairaudience.

I have a question for you, Pat. Are the gods merely part of our minds, or do they exist independently of our minds?

First of all, I would say that everything is Mind. The gods certainly existed in the minds of ancient civilizations and, when something is created in the mind, it definitely exists for those who created it. In one sense, Mind is outside time, as we understand it, but it is said that when a powerful mind-picture creates a thought-form of a god, the thought-form becomes inhabited by *that* for which it was formed or imagined.

I also think that the Godhead divided itself into two spheres – male and female – in order to create life itself. As many occult societies affirm, there exists the divine Male and Female Principles (God and Goddess), but only one Initiator, who is sexless – being neither male nor female – and utterly beyond our comprehension at this stage of our evolutionary progress. In the future, as we advance, the dawning of a new understanding will occur, I have no doubt.

And so, yes, I believe that the gods exist independently of our minds, but that each race of people identifies them in different ways, attributing to them various personality traits which are part of a particular race or country's character.

Demi-gods also exist. After a very long invocation to Hermes, and alone in the Circle, I confirm that I actually saw the head of the 'Messenger of the Gods' manifest above the Circle in marvellous astral colours, and wearing his silver helmet.

There are also those souls who have reached the Plane of Masterhood and may be regarded as 'gods'. These too are real and exist in their own sphere; having been purified through numerous rebirths, they have reached the Golden Land.

The practice of meditation is usually couched in mysterious terminology. Why is this, Patricia?

Most of what has been written about meditation is expressed in semi-religious terms, but meditation is an entirely personal practice and need not have anything to do with religion. Neither is it the prerogative of the Eastern races, where it is connected with Yoga, self-hypnosis and similar disciplines. Meditation is a method of self-development that can be practised by anyone regardless of any outside influences.

The techniques used are a way of exploring the *inner* mind, searching for what have been described as 'treasures'. These are beyond the mundanity of everyday existence. An echo of them is often experienced when a piece of music, a poem, or a special emotional happening occurs. The brain suddenly connects with the *inner* mind and the realization of another more glorious reality where all troubles vanish as if they had never been.

To attain this *true* state of being, there are only three necessary qualifications. The first is a belief that this is possible, that deep within the human being there is something wondrous to be discovered. The second is knowledge of how to retreat from the world into this *inner* reality. And thirdly the mandatory patience and persistence such a practice requires.

During meditation, the awareness leaves the World of Form. The eyes close upon it and the *inner* vision becomes what it actually is, the true state of consciousness. In this state it is possible to envisage and deliberately create positive thought-forms with which to enhance the outer physical life.

This *inner* world gives comfort, peace and privacy; it is a place to gain respite and a renewal of the confidence necessary for facing the tasks of life. Contact with this spiritual, and most important part of Self-hood bestows, in no small way, enlightenment and wisdom.

Patricia, have you heard of the 'Hand of Fatima'? I bought one on holiday abroad, but do not know what it represents. Can you help?

This talisman is said to represent the hand of Fatima, Mohammed's daughter, but symbols of hands appear in other parts of the world, most of them being associated with protection and divine grace.

Although this particular hand is known in Islamic cultures as the 'Hand of Fatima', and in Jewish lore as the 'Hand of Miriam', its origins go far back into the mists of time when the Goddess ruled these Middle Eastern lands. Originally, it was the hand of the Goddess warding off all evil, especially the Evil Eye.

In pre-Islamic Arabia, the feminine principle of divinity was undoubtedly revered as the Goddess Threefold – of the threefold moon – and in this form was present in the black stone of the Kaaba at Mecca. The sacred spring at Mecca has long been connected with the worship of the Goddess, and the crescent moon which is Her symbol still adorns the Islamic flag.

There is ample archaeological evidence to confirm that this downward-pointing Hand predates both Islam and Judaism; and suggests that its provenance is cultural rather than religious. It is known in Islamic countries as *Hamsa* – Arabic for five digits – and certainly has long been recognized as an ancient talisman for averting evil, or granting protection, as the case might be. A common sight in the Middle East, the symbol is incorporated in charms, amulets, cars, and jewellery for this purpose. Often, the Hand is stylized and made of silver or silver-gilt and inset with semi-precious stones or decorated with delicate designs – even the six-pointed Star of David. The Hand of Fatima I once purchased is of the latter type. They are made to hang downwards with a metal ring at the 'wrist' part of the Hand.

Could you please tell me how you view fairies? Do you believe they exist, or are they just another product of the imagination?

I have always kept an open mind concerning fairies, in fact any subject which has not been proved or disproved. Sir James Barrie, who wrote *Peter Pan*, did so because he had actually seen fairies or 'little folk' as some people call them. I read somewhere that a lady actually saw what she considered to be a fairy. This was in Ireland on a walking holiday. She stopped to rest on the bank of a river, enjoying the scenery and gazing around, then closed her eyes for a few minutes. Rested, and ready to leave, she glanced across at the opposite bank and saw a very small individual sitting on a rock. He was wearing a tunic and trousers of red and green, with a little floppy hat, and appeared to be fishing. The lady instinctively leaned forward, rubbed her eyes, and looked again, but he had vanished.

I occasionally hear other similar stories and cannot dismiss them all as being made up or imagined. For example, we know that there was once a race of very small people, but they were made of flesh and blood like the rest of us, and were called the Little People, or the Little Folk. Their dwellings have been discovered in Ireland, the Isle of Man, and the north of Scotland. They would appear and disappear with alarming alacrity and so were thought to be non-human and belonging to realms other than the material world. There was a simple reason for this apparent feat of dematerialization. Their homes were underground with an entrance in the roof of what looked like a grassy mound. When they vanished from sight, they had merely dropped down into their dwelling, which from a distance could not be seen.

These Little People, although very small, were strong and energetic, and over the centuries gradually intermingled with what we today consider to be normal-sized people. I believe that my own paternal grandmother was a descendant of the Little Folk, as she was quite small and petite, and her sister likewise. Their maiden name was Machin, a name which means 'fairy' or 'elf', and in Sheffield there is an elevated area called Machin Bank, or Fairy Bank.

The Leprechaun or Fairy Shoe-maker, whose gold you may win if you keep a tight hold on him, is only one of a vast hierarchy of elemental beings which inhabit Irish folklore. These Irish fairies can be roughly divided into two main groups named locally as the 'gregarious' and the 'solitary'. The former align with the Little People and are considered to be descendants of the Firbolg, an ancient Irish race. They are the ones who lived (or live) underground. The 'solitary' could well be a name for fairies of a more ethereal kind, such as those spirits called the 'Sidhe' (pronounced 'Shee'), meaning 'of the hills', which link with the ancient race known as the Tuatha de Danaan – the 'People of Danu'. Danu or Dana was the Mother Goddess of these people, who, when they had disappeared into history, became gods themselves. The Tuatha de Danaan were also legendary for their magical and shape-shifting abilities. They were tall people, very beautiful, with long golden hair and blue eyes which burned with an inner fire. Alas, they were driven into the Hollow Hills by their conquerors, the Milesians, and eventually passed into what some call the Summerland of the Astral Plane where they dwell as the Shining Ones. They left behind the products of their artistic skills in the inscriptions and wonderful intricate patterns engraved in stone, as well as bronze spear-heads exquisitely worked. Fiona Macleod (the pen name of William Sharp) sang of them in 'The Immortal Hour', thus:

How beautiful they are,
The lordly ones,
Who dwell in the hills,
In the hollow hills . . .
Their limbs are more white
Than shafts of moonshine:
They are more fleet
Than the March wind . . .

The dreaded Bean Sidhe (ban shee), or 'Woman of the Hills', is a hideous old hag who is said to appear, uttering frightful wailing and keening sounds, to presage a death. When young and apparently healthy people die suddenly, the Irish peasants used to believe that they had been taken by the fairies to become their husbands or wives, the dead bodies being false ones deposited in their place. Babies were often carried off by the fairies, who left a weak fairy changeling in exchange. However, it is believed that many of these people have been recovered from the fairies, and the way this was done is as follows:

On Hallowe'en, stand at a crossroads or a place indicated by a witch, for on this night all the fair hills open and the 'Hosting of the Sidhe' occurs. Riders race across the night sky – their horses whinnying and sweating beneath them. As the host sweeps past with a spell-bound man, woman or child, a sudden gust of wind tells you that now is the time to throw either dust or milk at the riders, and the wind will make sure it covers them. The fairies must at once surrender the one who you are seeking.

Now, do *you* believe in fairies?

How do you construct a Magic Mirror?

I presume you mean a Black Mirror, as mirrors used for the development of clairvoyance are nearly always black. Constructing one is fairly easy. Firstly, you must obtain a circular piece of convex glass. Ideally, the glass cover from a clock face is what you require, so look in the *Yellow Pages* for a clockmaker. I'm sure you will be able to purchase one quite reasonably from such a source. Or you may even secure this item from someone who owns an old broken clock. The diameter should be around five inches, although a larger piece of glass can be used if desired. Then, it is a matter of painting the *convex* side of the glass with matt-black paint. This will need two separate coats to obtain the necessary opaque appearance. Allow the first coat of paint to dry thoroughly before applying the second.

Now, you need to mount the glass in a suitable frame. A wooden one would be the best. Decorate it by painting your own symbols upon it, but don't use any bright or garish colours. You could paint the frame silver, with any symbols painted black or, alternatively, you can set the mirror in a shallow bowl or plate painted in a similar fashion. It all depends upon what is available and what feels right to you.

When your mirror is quite ready, it should be bathed in moonlight for at least three nights, being careful that only the Moon sees it. When it is not in use, it is vital that you wrap the mirror in a black velvet cloth so that it is not exposed to daylight.

You must remember that every tool used to aid clairvoyance is only an ordinary piece of equipment. It has no magic in it *per se*; it only becomes magical when you begin to use it for the above reason – and, most importantly, it begins to work for you. As soon as you have made the mirror, you must dedicate it in your own words and/or according to the particular path upon which you are working. A Black Mirror can be used by anyone, regardless of their beliefs, and on a purely mental level, if they are intent upon developing clairvoyance in this manner.

I presume that, as you have asked me how to construct such a mirror, you need to know the best ways to use it. There are certain conditions which have to be observed. First of all, you should approach your initial working, and all your subsequent workings, in an attitude of quiet optimism and with an open mind. It is also very important to be in a good mood, as nothing will be gained from sitting if you are in a bad one. You may see nothing at all for the first few times, but you must not lose hope or enthusiasm. Like any other training you may embark upon, it must be learned, and it takes time.

Keeping a record of your 'sittings' is a must, even if you see nothing. You should record your feelings and impressions and even small occurrences while you were thus engaged. The phase of the moon should be duly recorded, and after a while you may find that a particular phase is more conducive to receiving visions than another. The prevailing weather conditions may seem unimportant to the undertaking, but nevertheless will have an effect upon your mind and body. And, of course, it is very necessary to feel comfortable at these sessions by wearing the right clothing – nothing too tight or restricting in any way. The room, also, should be at a temperature which is comfortable, neither too cold nor too stuffy, and of course will be in darkness, except for a candle placed somewhere away from the 'speculum', so that the flame does not reflect in it.

Do remember not to sit for too long at first. Fifteen minutes is quite long enough at the beginning; the time may be gradually lengthened as you progress. A few breathing exercises can be employed before you begin, as these will help you to relax. Whatever you 'see', you will be able to evaluate in time, and recognize whether the visions come to you from the 'Gate of Horn' – that of true clairvoyance, true sight – or the 'Gate of Ivory', which gives unclear and sometimes chaotic 'scenes' that are best ignored. Differentiating the value of what you 'see' is all part of becoming a genuine clairvoyant.

Mrs Crowther, I have often wondered about the figure of Britannia, as seen on British currency. Is she related to the witches' Goddess in any way?

Yes. Britannia *is* our Goddess: they are one and the same. In the *Encyclopaedia Britannica* it states that Britannia is a Romano-British goddess. Not so! She was hoary with age before Rome was even built. It is true, however, that the Romans based some of their coinage upon existing coinage minted by the Phoenician 'Barats' of Lycaonia.

The Phoenicians occupied the seaboard of Lebanon and Syria, north of Mount Carmel. Their main cities were Tyre, Sidon and Byblos, and their exports included Tyrian purple dye and cloth, furniture (from the timber of Lebanon), and jewellery. To these people, who were inveterate seafaring traders and artisans, Britannia was known as Barati – 'Mistress of the Waves', and the 'Holy Lady of the Waters'. They came to Albion, the 'White Island', as Britain was then known, around 2800 BC and we traded our wares with them which included lead, copper, wool, hides, iron and tin.

Before the rise of patriarchal religions, the Goddess was worshipped throughout Europe and the Middle East, and in most parts of the world, so of course She was known to the Phoenicians. Her names differed according to country and even locality. One of the earliest for Her in Britain was An or Annis, while the male deity or Horned God was known as Al. So the name 'Alan', being a combination of both, is very ancient indeed.

187

The Celts knew the Goddess variously as Bridget, Brit and Bride, until eventually the name 'Brit-Annis' came into being, which evolved into 'Britannia'.

The Goddess first appeared on coins in Britain under Hadrian, and in the reign of Charles II Britannia was modelled by one of his mistresses, the Duchess of Richmond. But when Queen Anne came to the throne, the old figure was discarded in favour of a sharper, high-relief design in which the bare leg of Britannia was covered up, reportedly on the orders of the Queen.

Britannia was seen personified as a goddess. Early portraits depict her wrapped in a white garment with her right breast exposed. She was usually seated on a rock amidst the waves, holding a spear, with a shield propped beside her and a light-house behind – a symbol of her sacred fire.

The Victoria era still portrayed Britannia as a young woman with golden hair, wearing her Corinthian helmet and her white robes. Her shield, however, which once depicted the male sun-cross of St George within the 'female' shield, now held the British Union Flag. And she was no longer bare-breasted, prob-ably due to the modesty of Victorian society. Another rather amusing change occurred. Originally, Britannia's spear rested between her thighs, but over the years it was gradually moved further away from that position and eventually placed in front of her knees.

In the nineteenth century, Benedetto Pistrucci, a new designer at the British Mint, turned Britannia to face right for the first time ever, while another engraver, Wyon, put the rose, thistle and shamrock in the exergue beneath the figure, repre-senting England, Scotland and Ireland. More changes occurred over the course of time. Britannia was given a sheaf of corn to hold, as the Mother of Agriculture; the spear changed into a trident; and a lion appeared sitting beside her. The Lion is the national animal of England and is also featured on the Arms of Scotland. It was introduced in 1969 by Christopher Ironside when Britannia graced the 50p coin – as she still does at the time of writing. She also continues to be portrayed on British bank notes, but has gradually become smaller in size. The figure now appears on the £10 note in a silver hologram; on the latest £20 note Britannia is placed in a corner in a circle half an inch in diameter. Using my magnifying glass, I can see that this design is an early one in which the Goddess has one leg exposed and is holding a sheaf of corn in her right hand. Her spear rests at her left side and her shield holds the cross of St George.

A fine statue of Britannia standing with the British Lion can be seen in Plymouth, and a carved figure of her, 5 foot high, from the time of the Yorkshire clan of the Brigantes, can be viewed at the National Museum in Edinburgh.

N.B. Since writing the above, it has been announced that the figure of Britannia is to be banished from British coinage, along with the traditional heraldic designs, including the crowned lion, on a total of seven coins. To deliberately erase Britain's titular Goddess in this manner is a blatant attempt to destroy the country's history. Britannia has been an enduring symbol of the pride and spirit of the British people for almost two thousand years and, like the Union Jack, represents Britain's unique freedom-loving and democratic character. Words from Alan V. Insole's book *Immortal Britain* come to mind:

When a land neglects her legends
Sees but falsehood in the past
And its people view their sires
In the light of fools or liars,
'Tis a sign of its decline.
Branches that but blight their roots
Yield no sap for lasting fruits.

Most of the famous occult systems in the Western world have been written about and discussed ad nauseam *and, although I know they are very worthwhile and admirable systems to follow, I feel the need to explore something 'new' or perhaps expressed differently. Do I make sense, Patricia? Anyway, I wondered if you knew of an occultist who fits the bill, or whose writings would make a refreshing change?*

I don't know if you have ever come across the writings of Melita Denning and Osborne Phillips? They wrote a series of five books entitled *The Magical Philosophy*, published in 1975. The work *does* cover the Qabalah, but so much more than has been written hitherto. As stated in the book: 'This is the definitive work on the Western Mystery Tradition – both setting forth the way mainstream Western occultism has developed and providing a completely modern and psychologically valid re-statement of the Magical Art . . .'

There is also an astrologer and psychic I would draw to your attention; although his books are now very rare, they are not unattainable. He was born in 1826 in Wales, and his name was John Thomas, but he was known as Charubel. He was a close friend of Alan Leo and an associate of other astrologers, particularly for one of his books, *The Degrees of the Zodiac Symbolised*, which became the most popular referred to work on the subject. Charubel was well known throughout England but shunned the limelight. He became a curative Mesmerist and was a renowned Welsh seer and mystic, studying herbalism, mediumship and occultism.

In 1891 Charubel's health began to fail and he was unable to contribute further to the *Astrologer's Magazine*. Not having been interested in money during his lifetime, he found himself penniless and relying upon the bounty of others. Confined to his room, the world came to him. Visitors appeared from every part of the globe, all occultists of some description, who travelled to study at the feet of Charubel, regarded as a great teacher. He died in 1908 in Manchester.

I am sure you would find much of interest in at least one of Charubel's titles, *The Psychology of Botany, Minerals and Precious Stones*, published in 1906, and will be able to locate it from the archive department of your local library. The book is described as 'A Treatise on Trees, Shrubs, Plants, Minerals and Precious Stones for the cure of ailments of the Human System without medicine but by Sympathy – positive and negative – on the Soul Plane, by Charubel the Great Seer. A Collegian who trained for the Gospel 60 years ago and gave his whole life up for the love of Nature and the study of the Supernatural Elements'.

Charubel discovered the existence of a personal and direct link between the soul of an individual and the souls of plants, trees and minerals. He also found that these had the power to heal when their auras were attuned to a person who needed assistance or healing. Over a period of many years, the seer discovered the sacred names and magical seals of certain trees, shrubs, minerals, plants and precious stones which exist on what he named the 'Plane of Soul'. These names and seals were revealed to him, and it is these which unlock the healing power. Charubel covers many species from the botanical and the mineral kingdoms in this great work.

There are at least fifty magical invocations within the book's pages, which cover practically all physical and mental disorders, with accompanying discourse revealing the significance of their hidden virtues. And the seer ends his work with these words:

I, Charubel, am the ordained instrument to publish to this race, now in the sear of its life, this divine philosophy. However you may feel disposed to treat this subject depend on it there is no other messenger born nor yet within the folds of a distant future, who will publish again this philosophy, further than he or she who may seek to call the attention of the world to what I have written.

From all the invocations contained in this book, I have chosen those which I feel will be most helpful and beneficial to my readers in the present day.

The Invoking Rituals

These truths to me have long been given,

By sages on earth whose lives are in heaven,
This teaching of Nature I give here to you,
Is celestial wisdom, received by the few.

The method Charubel used for invocation and which appeared to
him on the Soul Plane is contained in the following process:

First, decide upon the tree, plant, shrub, mineral or precious
stone which connects with your problem and whose assistance you
desire to invoke. You must then visualize this for a short period, in
its actual and earthly form. Then, still concentrating, transform it on
to the Soul, or Astral, Plane, seeing it as a divine symbol. And, when
the time seems right to you, pronounce its sacred name.

Here are some examples.

Monks Hood *for colds, chills, influenza and acute infections*

While concentrating upon the divine symbol, repeat the invoca-
tionary word six times, deliberately and reverentially. After two
hours, repeat this a second time, if necessary. A warm glow
succeeds the chill.

The sacred name
LU-VAR-MEL
The divine symbol

Wood Sorrel *for all types of cancer*

This plant is a life-giver, a vitalizer. While meditating upon this small plant, entreat its aid by repeating its sacred name and it will glide, like some sweet angel, into your room. Repeat this sacred name and concentrate upon its divine symbol morning and night.

The sacred name
AV-VIR-EVEL
The divine symbol

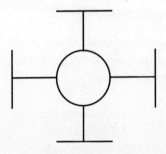

Copper *for strengthening psychic protection and giving moral courage*

When in need of such help repeat the following invocation once:

O thou who ridest on yonder constellation by thy name of Av-mah-hu-jah, clothe me in thy armour. Shield me with thy head, watch me with thine eye. Make me strong in thee and in the power of thy might. Amen.

The sacred name
AV-MAH-HU-JAH
The divine symbol

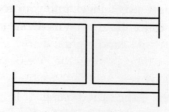

The Ruby *for grief, bereavement, disappointment and all who are oppressed*

The hidden virtues of this precious stone will attract to itself the burden of your sorrow. Look to its divine symbol and its sacred name and repeat it nine times.

The sacred name
DER-GAB-EL
The divine symbol

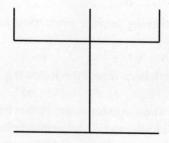

Do you think that animals have souls, Mrs Crowther?

I am sure that animals *do* have souls or spirits because they have feelings and can think for themselves. They are on a lower level of the Tree of Life, but are able to communicate with their own kind and, if domesticated, can express themselves to their owners through their particular vocabularies and their actions. Animals surely have their place in the World of Spirit, and after death pass on to the Lower Astral Plane.

The fact that there are countless cases of owners seeing their pets again after they have died must be proof enough that they continue in spirit. When they appear to those who have loved them, what people see are the astral bodies of the animals, through which, as with human beings, their spirits continue to exist in a finer form.

I have discussed my own experiences on this type of manifestation elsewhere, but the most recent one occurred after the passing of Smut, a dearly loved female cat, and sister to Shah, who incidentally has just past his twentieth year! Smut had developed a tumour in her stomach which caused it to extend like a huge ball. She had various tests but all to no avail, and she was clearly limited in her habits and unable to climb the stairs to sleep on her favourite bed. And so, after many harrowing deliberations, she was given peace. I mention all this for what was to follow.

About a week later, my partner, Ian, was retrieving something from the fridge in the kitchen, when he suddenly sprang backwards. I happened to see him from the next room, and asked what was wrong. He said, 'You will not believe this!' Then he told me that the shape of a black cat had run past between him and the fridge. He had automatically jumped back at this sudden and unexpected occurrence. We reasoned that the speed of the apparition could have been due to the fact that Smut no longer had the awful swelling and was now free to run fast again.

I think there is a difference between domestic animals who

have a loving family of humans around them and live in comfortable warm homes, and livestock which are accustomed to living and being with other animals. I rather think that these animals, and other herd animals in the wild, have group souls. They do not receive individual attention and love and, living as a herd, are not given the opportunity to develop separate and special characteristics of their own. Livestock, of course, are kept largely to be killed and eaten. Nevertheless, I am convinced that all living creatures have astral bodies and therefore a continuance in spirit.

As you know, Patricia, I have been a lone worker for several years and I am wondering what I should do about my magical tools and my Book of Shadows when I leave this Earth. What would you suggest?

If you know of a coven, or a member of a coven, you could leave your tools to them, so that when the need arises they could be given to a new initiate of that coven in the same way that my friend, Jean MacDonald, passed her Grand Mother's athame to me. Of course, they would have to be well cleansed of your aura and reconsecrated to the new witch. Old ritual tools possess much power, having been worked with for a long time, and I can certainly confirm this statement regarding the athame that was sent to me. As Jean said, it had been consecrated in the past and used in magical workings for many years, so was imbued with a great deal of power.

Another way, failing the above, would be to leave your tools to Graham King, the owner of the Museum of Witchcraft at Boscastle in Cornwall. This would avoid them falling into the wrong hands or even being destroyed, and Graham would surely display them. However, leaving them to a witch would obviate any mishandling and ensure that, in the course of time, another witch would use them.

What you must do immediately, however, is to put into your Will exactly whom you wish to have your tools. This is vital, as verbal promises, etc. are not enough to ensure that what you want to happen to them will occur. The only way you can be absolutely certain your wishes will be carried out is through your Last Will and Testament.

Regarding your *Book of Shadows*, this is a slightly different problem. It should be bequeathed to a High Priestess or High Priest of the Craft as it may contain material that only a Third Degree initiate should possess. If, for any reason, this is not possible, then the best thing to do is to burn it, when you feel the time has come for this to be done. However, in the case of a sudden death this should also be entered into your Will and your executor will perform his or her duty apropos your wishes. If you had already burned the book during your lifetime, it does not matter, but in case of unforeseen circumstances your wishes should still be inserted in your Will.

I hope that I have been of some help to you with this problem.

Are you a vegetarian and/or do you follow a strict diet before a meeting? And do you think certain foods are beneficial or otherwise to the development of psychic abilities?

I do not eat meat, red or white, but do have fish, so cannot call myself a true vegetarian. I do, however, follow a strict diet before entering the Circle. This consists of light, easily digestible meals, during that particular day; carbohydrate-rich foods – pasta or rice dishes. I avoid fried foods as they are slow to digest and may produce indigestion during a ritual. Any form of alcohol is also a no-go area.

Certain foods are detrimental to psychic development – especially meat which in my opinion may contain etheric vestiges of the terror that an animal has experienced before slaughter. Factory farming conditions themselves, in which thousands of animals exist, create feelings of stress or unease. Beneficial foods for psychic development are those based upon Vegan principles, i.e. fruit, vegetables, cereals and legumes. These supply nutrients in a balanced way and have no connection with the suffering of animals. Alcohol in moderation is acceptable, but over-indulgence affects the brain as well as the body's organs and would inhibit psychic progress. Similarly, the use of drugs may induce short-term psychicism but this effect is ephemeral and not a true and natural development of the Sixth Sense.

Why are some numbers considered to be sacred?

Actually, odd numbers are considered to be more sacred than even ones and there are many reasons why they are thought of in this way. My own feelings in this regard pertain to the fact that odd numbers cannot be divided equally, and because of this there is an extra numeral which may have symbolized the presence of a spiritual dimension. There is only one Sun in the sky giving light and life and, in some religions, only one god, so the number one became a potent and sacred number. It could be that this number represented God (and/or the Sun), and so was thought to be present in all odd numbers. The Pagans of old believed very strongly in the power of odd numbers, and the Roman poet Virgil wrote: *Numero Deus impare guader*, 'God delights in odd numbers.'

Other, more prosaic interpretations of odd numbers, yet nonetheless sacred ones, may reside in certain phenomena people saw around them, such as a couple – man and woman – who brought forth a child hence the number three. The Moon appeared to people in different guises – waxing, full and waning phases which were understood to represent the Goddess Triformis in Her role of Maiden, Mother and Crone. In Christianity, the trinity is expressed as Father, Son and Holy Ghost, while occult philosophers adhered to the premise that humans were composed of three bodies, the physical, etheric and spiritual. Nature, too, has three kingdoms – animal, vegetable and mineral. Alchemists identified three principles in their Art – salt, sulphur and mercury, while the Druids expressed much of their wisdom in triads, their most important symbol being the 'Tribann' – the Three Rays of Light.

The number seven has always carried great respect and reverence. The ancients recognized seven planets. These included the Sun and the Moon, although today they are known as luminaries. They called them the 'Seven Sacred Planets' and they were acknowledged in the following order: Saturn, Jupiter, Mars, Sun, Venus, Mercury, Moon. In the science of astrology, these Sacred Seven were considered to rule or empower all Earthly things. For thousands of years, the number seven has been incorporated in innumerable mystical symbols and signs. The importance of it cannot be too strongly stressed. In astrology, seven is the number of Saturn and carries a deeply spiritual and karmic influence within it. In a birth chart, the 'Saturn Return', when the planet has travelled through all the signs and returned to the place it occupied at the native's birth (which takes approximately 29½ years), signifies an important change or happening in the native's life. Saturn always introduces some kind of transformation which the native is born to experience in their lifetime. This will occur at any time between the Return and the native's age of thirty-four years – 3 + 4 = 7. There are many allusions to seven in the Bible, including the Seven Deadly Sins, and the Seven Sacraments, while Pagan cultures celebrated the Seven Wonders of the World.

Nine was also significant as being the number of moons required for a baby to be born; perhaps because of this it has a definite link with beginnings and endings. In occultism, it was the magical number of the Moon long before it was found that the orb measures 2,160 miles across, numbers which when added together come to nine. So nine, with its powerful association with the Moon and the Moon Goddess, is used frequently in witchcraft and the magical arts: one ancient spell for example is named, 'The White Mare and her Ninefold'.

An odd number *par excellence* is of course thirteen. And in witchcraft and other mystical groups it has been recognized down the ages as being of supreme importance. The most magical use of this number was in the group of twelve plus the leader.

Sometimes, the thirteenth member was not of the flesh, but the invisible spiritual leader or deity to whom the group's magical work and way of life was dedicated. In the Craft of the Wise, the leader is the High Priestess who is able to commune with the Goddess. The High Priest, likewise, is empowered by the Horned God. This sacred number also has links with the Moon, as in most years there are thirteen lunar months, and in Celtic and Nordic traditions each Full Moon has a special name. There are various lists of these names according to the culture and climate of a particular country, but in most northern climes, and beginning at the Vernal Equinox, the Full Moons are recognized as follows: Awakening Moon, Grass Moon, Planting Moon, Rose Moon, Lightning Moon, Harvest Moon, Hunters Moon, Blood Moon, Tree Moon, Long Night Moon, Ice Moon, Snow Moon and Death Moon.

What is the difference between superstition and magic?

Superstitions mostly arise from associations with either positive or negative events. Salt, for example, was once a valuable commodity in some countries, so when someone spilt it, usually by accident, it was considered to be bad luck. To avert the threatened misfortune, the person who had spilled the salt immediately took a pinch of it between finger and thumb and threw it over their left shoulder. The first cuckoo calling signified the arrival of Spring. This was a positive occurrence and also a good sign for whoever heard it. Breaking a mirror was bad luck for the one who broke it, in fact seven years' bad luck. This was chiefly because mirrors have always been implements of divination, so to break one was thought of as disastrous: the means of knowing the will of the gods had been destroyed. The person's own reflection had been shattered too, so a sign of ill luck to come.

Omens of one kind or another are as old as time itself and were often supposed to indicate destiny. Therefore, an owl hooting in the middle of the night close to your home, or even on one of your window-sills, is not the *cause* of any bad luck, it is merely acting as a messenger to warn you of some trouble to come – and forewarned, is forearmed. Superstitions and omens have become so ingrained in people's consciousness that many of them are still observed today. Omens were once thought of as the force of magic operating in the world: some evil entity at work intent upon causing all manner of harm to unfortunate believers.

Magic, however, has no connection with superstition or minds determined to read portents in everything secular. Magic is a conscious human effort to change existing circumstances for the better, or as Aleister Crowley succinctly put it, 'The art of causing change to occur in conformity with the Will.'

Appendix: General Guidelines

These are intended to complement the Laws of the Craft and help the smooth running of the coven.

The Magic Circle

Before entering the Circle, everyone should take a bath with a portion of salt added to the water. The bath may be taken by the members in their own homes before arriving at the covenstead, but they must don a complete set of clean clothing after taking the bath.

Within the Circle, all females must wear a conspicuous necklace of beads or gemstones which are *all the same size*. It must encircle the base of the neck, and look like a *circle*. This is because the Goddess wears one, and because it signifies the *circle of rebirth*. No other additional necklaces or long chains should be worn. They would look incongruous and completely spoil the effect of the magical necklace. The High Priestess should keep a few spare, purified necklaces handy, just in case a female forgets to bring hers. (It has been known!) When not in use, the necklace should be kept in a little velvet bag and away from everyday items. The necklace is blessed and purified when its owner is initiated.

Smoking in the Circle is strictly prohibited.

Wine should be decanted and placed under or near the altar before the Circle is cast.

The Circle should be exactly 9 feet in diameter, no more, no less. The altar stands in the centre of the Circle, facing North. If members are few and cannot join hands for the circumambulations, the altar may be moved into the North part of the Circle, but it must be repositioned later, and before the Circle is closed. A way to avoid moving the altar at all is for the witches to hold a cord between two of them, or two cords between four witches, if necessary, while circling takes place. It is entirely a matter of preference.

A word here about the Circle itself. I have visited two covensteads where the actual Magic Circle was nowhere to be seen. Stones had been arranged in a circle instead. I could not believe my eyes. Never before had I known that white, noticeable, foundation of the Craft, and indeed other ancient forms of Ritual Magic, to be absent or substituted by anything. Nothing can replace the *white circular ring* for the building of the Magical Cosmos, either painted upon the floor, or achieved by a length of white rope laid down over a carpet. If the former, a circular, rubber-backed carpet can be placed *within* the Circle, leaving the painted ring *in view*.

The white circle of demarcation, of Magic, of knowing that you are 'Between the Worlds', a clear, unbroken, continuous line, without beginning or ending, and therefore a *visible* reminder of where you are, simply cannot be improved upon in any shape or form. Those witches who attempt to change this time-honoured and hallowed concept of the Magical Arts, makes me wonder how they came to be initiated in the first place.

If it is really desired for stones to be at the covenstead (which hopefully have not been filched from a sacred site) they can be placed *outside* the Magic Circle, but certainly not instead of it.

Erecting the Circle

The High Priestess of the coven is the only witch to form and raise the Magic Circle. The exceptions here are if the High

Priestess cannot be present, when the Maiden, or a female witch, can perform this task. Another is when a High Priest, for whatever reason, has no magical partner, and wishes to initiate a female with whom to work and/or start a new coven. After his new partner has been initiated, she will henceforth be instructed how to form the Circle and also close it. A lone male, if working in a coven, may also practise privately, on his own.

Dancing or Treading the Mill is performed deosil or sunwise. The exception here is when the work is performed to banish any hostile vibrations or negative forces, when the Dance can be reversed to circling Widdershins, or against the Sun. This type of working is best done when the Moon is waning. As the Moon gradually disappears, she takes with her the negative influences, thus aiding the rite.

While the Circle is raised and the meeting in progress, a witch may have to leave it for a genuine and/or urgent reason. There has been talk of making 'doorways' with athames for the witch to leave, and possibly return, but the simplest and indeed the safest way is to redraw the Circle with the athame or the Magic Sword, remembering that only the High Priestess, the High Priest or those who are working in the Second Degree may touch this instrument. The above rule also applies if the Circle is accidentally broken by someone's hand or in some other way. It should be redrawn immediately.

Candles

It is usual to have two candles of the same colour upon the altar (unless a particular rite demands more or less). This makes for harmony and looks right. The nature of the occasion informs as to what colour is used, unless The Rite of the Moon, or another rite for the Goddess Triformis, is to be performed. Then, the three colours of the Triple Goddess are displayed – Red, White and Dark Blue. Black candles can be employed for rites of a Saturnian nature. Plain white candles are perfectly acceptable if coloured ones are not available. They will give an old-world atmosphere of long ago.

The candles at the Four Gates of the Circle, if coloured, should depict the Four Basic Elements: Yellow or White at the East; Red or Orange at the South; Blue or Pale Green for the West; and Brown, Black or Dark Green in the North.

Before the Circle is cast, the candles upon the altar are lit, followed by those at the Gates, in this order – East, South, West and North. These tasks should be performed by the Maiden or Server of the coven. Otherwise, by the High Priestess or the High Priest.

At the end of the meeting, the candles are snuffed out in *reverse* order. The candles at the Gates are attended first – North, West, South and East, followed by those upon the altar. If a candle is to remain lit for any purpose, it should be placed in a safe position, ideally in a cauldron.

Candles which burn out or are accidentally extinguished must be immediately replaced or re-lit. If these are at the Gates, the Circle is broken then redrawn. A candle-snuffer is best for dealing with candle flames.

Charcoal is ignited before the commencement of a meeting and, if ignited from a candle flame, this candle should not be used in the rites. When it is well alight, a reliable person is chosen to tend the incense and make sure it is not too heavy in small rooms. It is worthwhile investing in properly made incense of a superior quality, as this substance will be penetrating the lungs during the ceremony. Great care must be taken when purchasing or making incense. Joss sticks are a popular and easy alternative, but whatever kind of incense is used, ensure that the room is adequately ventilated. Over a number of years, the walls will accumulate a deposit of soot.

The purpose of incense is to raise and inflame the mental perceptions of the coveners in accordance with the type of ritual being worked. It is a valuable aid to ritual, meditation, or prayer. It should be used with discrimination at all times. If you don't have good occult suppliers, you can try church incense. It has been found to be of a good quality and can be purchased at Catholic church supply shops.

Ritual

Rituals are best conducted after sundown and when the Moon is in her *new* or *Full* phases. One of the most important times is of course the Full Moon, or 'The Goddess 15'. This is the time *par excellence* for the working of magic: The Goddess 15, one lunation, for she is then symbolic of the point of turning back, creating as she does so, the 16th kala of supreme elixir. At the time of the Full Moon, the Moon should be drawn down into the body of the High Priestess. That is to say, the 15th kala or vibration of the Goddess is transferred to the body of the High Priestess. Therefore, it is necessary for her to be purified several times before 'Drawing down the Moon' occurs.

Rituals should not be changed or adulterated by coven members. This would be an insult to our forebears and to the person who initiated you and trusted you enough to allow you to copy from the Book of Shadows. Everything in it was put there for a reason, and only the foolish would consider that they know better than the witches of old. Missing anything out of a magical ritual might mean something going missing from that person's life. One cannot monkey with magic and get away with it.

Most covens today keep a separate book for the Degrees, Handfasting, Wiccaning and Passing Rites. These are the property of the leaders of a coven and are passed on when a witch gains the Third Degree.

If new rituals are added to the Book of Shadows, they should be identified as such, together with their source and/or author, and the date they were inserted. They should never be presented as part of the original material and tradition. A wise witch will adhere to the old ways and build upon them. The descendants of a coven must be aware of any additional material – and its source. The most beautiful poetry has been written for the God and Goddess over the last fifty years and has surely earned a place in the Book of Shadows but, again, be sure to include the poet's name under any insertions. New material should not replace the original, but complement and enhance it.

There seems to be some confusion in certain parts of the Craft, especially in recent years, concerning the *order* in which different actions are performed when casting the Circle. I will give the correct order as concisely as possible, including the performance of subsequent actions together with how the Sheffield Coven disperses, after closing the Circle.

1. Banish any negative vibrations at the Four Gates thus: Draw a Banishing Pentagram with the athame, saying, 'Let all malignity and hindrance Depart! Depart! Depart!' Make three small circles, then stab the athame through them with the last three words.
2. Draw the Circle.
3. Consecrate the Water.
4. Asperge the Circle.
5. Purify the Circle with incense. Raising it at the Four Gates.
6. Greet the High Priest and all witches present.
7. Asperge everyone in the sign of the Degree in which they are working, then pass the incense in front of them three times. The High Priest repeats these actions on the High Priestess. (No. 7 is optional).
8. Invoke at the Four Gates with Horn or Bell, the High Priest showing the Pentacle to each Gate.
9. Purifications.
10. Prayers, etc.
11. Initial and obligatory circumambulation.
12. Rituals and reasons for the meeting, magical work, etc.
13. The ritual of Cakes and Wine. Sitting as witches for social intercourse and discussion. A time for friendship and humour.
14. Close the Circle.
15. Kisses exchanged between all present. Males clasp each other's hands.

16. Witches stand silently in a circle, each one meditating or communing with the Old Ones, for their own particular reasons.

17. All walk slowly round the Circle. On the third circuit, the first witch to pass the altar again bows to it then leaves the Circle. All others do likewise.

18. The Maiden (or Server) extinguishes the candles. The offerings and libations for the Earth are performed by the Maiden.

Temple Conduct

Within the Circle, the High Priestess should be addressed as 'my Lady' or by her Craft name, the High Priest as 'my Lord' or by *his* Craft name, as the leaders will. Other witches are addressed by their Craft names or, if working in the First Degree, by their birth names.

Craft names are never used outside the Circle. They are personal and private and should be kept so at all times, representing, as they do, a person's magical personality which is usually in the process of development. This name has nothing to do with the outside world; it should be treated with secrecy and silence. Like seeds which grow in darkness to become beautiful flowers in the sunlight, so it is with the magical personality.

A High Priestess or Witch Queen is always referred to as 'The Lady [name]', but a female of the Third Degree who is not (and never was) a working High Priestess of a coven would not be addressed in this way. A Witch Queen is a High Priestess (or former High Priestess) who has her own coven in which two separate initiates (male or female) have been elevated to the Third Degree, either by her own hands or by her High Priest's, and those two initiates have each formed new covens. Please note that the title 'Lady' is prefixed by the word 'The' in order to distinguish the title from the nobility of Europe. Therefore, the correct usage of the term within the Craft is 'The Lady . . .'

A Witch Queen's symbols of rank are a silver crown bearing a crescent moon, and a garter of blue or green velvet. This bears a silver buckle representing her own coven. Small, silver charms also decorate the garter, symbolizing each new coven formed by her initiates. These are usually presented to her by the coven concerned, and are highly valued by the Witch Queen as symbols of appreciation, good fellowship and remembrance. The silver bracelet is worn by a High Priestess or a Witch Queen, but by no other witch, because it is of special significance in the Craft of the Wise. It should bear the owner's Craft name in one of the magical alphabets, and also display the three Degrees of the Craft that the witch has passed through. A High Priest is entitled to wear a copper bracelet with similar embellishments. All females must display the Necklace of the Goddess. The necklace and the garter are of immeasurable age; the other decorations are of more recent origin.

The Magic Circle is a miniature cosmos, and in the Craft it is erected for the worship of the Great Goddess and Her Consort – the Great Horned God. Like any sacred sanctuary, it exists to sanctify the Earth and its people and has many magical uses, not least that of evoking the highest and purest qualities from within the Children of the Goddess.

On the very rare occasion of one or even two of the adherents displaying signs of animosity or distress of any kind, the Circle must be immediately closed and the matter discussed privately with the leaders. The negative thoughts and vibrations will have been felt by all, and no good could possibly come from attempting to continue the meeting.

The Magic Circle is often described as 'The Wood Between the Worlds', neither wholly in the spiritual nor the material world, but part of both. The Gods love to hear laughter and the sounds of their especial children enjoying themselves – 'Keep My Mysteries in Mirth!' So do not be afraid of letting your hair down in an appropriate part of the meeting.

A new initiate should be guided in the ways and rituals by an 'older' witch. The High Priestess must select that witch *before* the

Circle is erected, and no other witch may attempt to guide the new witch during the meeting.

If a member arrives at the covenstead in a bad frame of mind, tired, or under the influence of drink or drugs, they must not be allowed into the Circle, and they must be cautioned as to the seriousness of their behaviour. They should also be requested to attend a private discussion with the leaders concerning their problems. A female, if pregnant, must not be involved in any type of magical workings. The unborn child has no say as to whether it desires to be connected with witchcraft or not. Also, the magical vibrations and thought patterns of a rite, however well meant, may be impressed upon the embryo in its formation. *At this very important time, it needs only the protection of its mother's body.*

Visitors to the Covenstead

It is not advisable to invite witches from another coven to your meetings unless they are known and are familiar to you (no pun intended). Certainly, any person who presents themselves as a member of a genuine coven, or who informs you that they are a High Priest or High Priestess, *must not be allowed within the Circle.* It is just not worth the risk to the covenstead. If they *are* genuine, they will provide you with the name, address and telephone number of their initiator for you to confirm their claim. Even so, I doubt whether the members would be comfortable circling with a stranger as this is totally alien to Craft teachings. Of course, this kind of occurrence may never happen, but it is best to be aware of such things. Journalists have ingenious methods of gaining information, and are not above inveigling a friendly, young thing to gain entry into a coven. With strangers, however convincing, *always, but always, be on your guard.*

In earlier times, many covens met to celebrate the Greater Sabbats, with everyone enjoying each other's company. Today, we have more social gatherings which are gradually increasing in size.

But the general pattern of conferences, in which the standard diet consists of speakers, stalls and food, are becoming, in my opinion, a little stale. Of course, many witches and pagans continue to enjoy them; it is certainly an opportunity to meet up with friends and make new ones. But the carefree times when witches met to celebrate a special occasion on a grand scale, and everyone brought something to eat for the feast, seem to have vanished. Perhaps some covens are still able to meet in this way. I know that witches in the USA do, because there is so much more space in their great outdoors and they can hold their gatherings without any fear of interruptions. As they say, we live in a different age!

The Modern View?

'DIY' witches may scoff at keeping to the old ways, and perform their initiations from published books, but the thing that they fail to grasp is that *genuine* initiations are those bestowed by an *already initiated witch* in a line that goes back into the distant past. There is also the transference of psychic power. This is one of the most important aspects of a true initiation and one which carries solemn responsibilities and dedication to the Goddess and the God.

Today, there is a lot of 'dumbing down', a debilitating attitude to life and learning on all levels, and it seems to have crept into the Craft. Many of today's pagans appear to be attracted to the Craft for the wrong reasons. To them it seems glamorous and romantic and really rather fun. It is none of these things. The Mysteries are magnificent in their revelations of Selfhood, but they cannot be bought; and the Gods will not reveal Themselves to those who believe otherwise. There is a corrupting influence abroad in today's materialistic society in which people are taught that money will buy anything. Well, it will not! And adherents of the Craft know the truth of this. They also know that initiation into the Mysteries is earned the hard way, by work and discipline, which are an integral part of life's pattern and grant a wholesome inner satisfaction combined with spiritual enlightenment.

Mysteries grow from a nucleus of inspired souls who are moved to discover the powers within themselves. Some of the techniques we use in the Craft today may have been found accidentally but, if they brought results, the method would be added to the bulk of the knowledge. As they worshipped the Great Goddess above all other gods, the rites were performed in Her name. They would thus establish a magical link with Her in that the power raised would be given to the Goddess. This helped the Goddess to become stronger in Her own sphere, so that She became known in most parts of the world. They also discovered that She would grant their wishes, providing that they gave Her the power from their bodies to do this. Magic *will* work if one realizes these truths.

It was also realized that men and women have the seeds of Godhood within them. Most of the world religions know this, but some of them seek to keep their followers ignorant of the fact. It was more profitable for the people to believe that the priests alone could aid them in spiritual matters. Thus, they controlled the population and achieved worldly power. Money, gold and all kinds of riches poured into church coffers, mostly because the people thought it would save them a place in heaven. Of course, the act of taking away a human being's responsibility for his or her own soul was the worst crime of all. The Children of the Goddess know that it is nothing less than their behaviour in this life, and indeed previous lives, that determines the soul's State of Being in the World of Spirit.

The Coven and Initiations

When an initiation takes place, all coven members usually attend. They can be present in the Circle, or sit quietly outside the Circle in order to witness it. This matter must be discussed beforehand and the new initiate questioned as to whether they would prefer the ceremony to be witnessed by the entire coven, or only by the leaders and the Maiden (or Server). At such an important and serious time in their life, they are entitled to be considered as to *their* feelings in this matter. Much depends upon their personality, so it is crucial to know their opinion. A Second Degree elevation is witnessed solely by those witches who are already working in that Degree themselves, and they may assist by taking one of the roles in the drama, or helping in other ways.

Regarding an aspirant awaiting initiation, it has been found that a much longer period of time than the 'year and a day' is necessary in some cases. In fact I do not know where this time period, with regard to initiations, came from. I don't remember Gerald mentioning it, but he could have done. However, in my opinion, it should have a large question mark added to it. The time certainly should not be *shorter* than a year and a day, and very often needs to be longer. It all depends upon the character, personality and make up of the aspirant, and no two people have the same approach to initiation. An intellectual person may quickly assimilate what must be learned of the practical aspects of the Craft, yet may find difficulty in expressing themselves on emotional levels. An important point concerning this type of soul is whether they are able to suspend the analytical part of their mind in favour of true belief. If the aspirant is an emotional, eager soul, control and balance must be learned. And so on. Any haste in this matter would be most unwise for all concerned.

Let it be known that responsibility for entry into the Mysteries does not rest entirely with the leaders of a coven. Most of it lies with the aspirant. It is the aspirant who approached the leaders of the coven and requested to be instructed in the ways of the Craft – and to be initiated. So, if the leaders have done their best in training and aiding the would-be witch, and have also studied the person's character and perused their birth chart to ascertain their suitability, it is no fault of the leaders if the aspirant changes their mind and realizes it is not the path for them. No harm has been done.

However, in most circumstances, having taken initiation, the new witch will reveal how it awakened or stirred their inner, spiritual self and also seemed strangely familiar to them – or words to that effect. They usually have something positive to say about how it affected them. The way they express themselves is immaterial.

Courtesy

After a meeting has taken place, coven members should assist in the cleaning of the Circle and return it to the orderly condition it was in prior to the meeting. This can be done directly after the meeting, but witches are not really in the mood for cleaning then. It is a time for enjoyment, relaxation, and a feast. A good idea is to have a rota for each member to clean the Circle in turn – hopefully, the next day. Just because the Circle happens to be in the home of the High Priestess and/or High Priest does not mean that this work must be *their* responsibility. Each witch (including the leaders) is honour bound to do their share and perform the task willingly: cleaning the candlesticks, polishing the altar, sweeping the floor, or whatever requires doing at the time. They should be instructed that the work of cleaning the Circle and the preparations for a meeting *are of as much importance as the meeting itself.*

Work and worship go hand in hand. The performance of menial tasks was once a prerequisite of being taught even the most elementary part of any Mysteries. This was both psychological and beneficial, the aspirant realizing very quickly that knowledge must be worked for and won. It was not going to be handed to them on a plate. Therefore, when aspects of the Mysteries *were* revealed to them, they were regarded with even greater respect than if they had been granted more easily. To those who serve at the altar of the Goddess and the Horned One, these mundane activities give an innate feeling of well-being and satisfaction. They are duties performed with love.

Prayer to Isis

Holiest of the holy, perpetual comfort of mankind. You whose beautiful grace nourishes the whole world, whose heart turns towards all those in sorrow and tribulation as a mother's to her children; you who take no rest by night, no rest by day, but are always at hand to succour the distressed by land and sea, dispersing the gales that beat upon them. Your hand alone can disentangle the hopelessly knotted skeins of fate, terminate every spell of bad weather, and restrain the stars from harmful conjunction. The gods above adore you, the gods below do homage to you, you set the orb of heaven spinning around the poles, you give light to the sun, you govern the universe, you trample down the powers of hell. At your voice the stars move, the seasons recur, the spirits of earth rejoice, the elements obey. At your nod the winds blow, clouds drop wholesome rain upon the earth, seeds quicken, buds swell. Birds that fly through the air, beasts that prowl on the mountain, serpents that lurk in the dust, all these tremble in a single awe of you.

The remains of a temple of Isis were discovered in London and this prayer was found in a display of religious artefacts in the Cuming Museum of London History, Walworth Road, Southwark.

Bibliography

Albright, W.F., *The Archaeology of Palestine* (Penguin, 1956)

Bracelin, Jack, *Gerald Gardner – Witch!* (Octagon Press, 1960)

Charubel (John Thomas), *The Degrees of the Zodiac Symbolised* (Green, Nichols, 1898)

—, *The Psychology of Botany, Minerals and Precious Stones* (Welch, 1906. Reprinted as *Grimoire Sympathia*, IHO, 2003)

Chesterton, G.K., *The Collected Poems of G.K. Chesterton* (Methuen, 1936)

Claridge, Marcus, and Richardson, Alan, *The Old Sod, the Life of William G. Gray* (Ignotus Press, 2003)

Crowther, Patricia, *High Priestess* (Phoenix, 1999) (Originally published as *One Witch's World*, Hale, 1998)

—, *Lid off the Cauldron* (Muller, 1981)

—, *The Zodiac Experience* (Weiser, 1992)

Denning, Melita, and Phillips, Osborne, *The Magical Philosophy* (Llewellyn, 1975)

Farrar, Janet and Stewart, *The Witches' Way* (Hale, 1990)

Gardner, Gerald, *High Magic's Aid* (Houghton, 1949)

—, *Kris and other Malay Weapons* (Progressive, 1936 and EP, 1973)

Graves, Robert, *The White Goddess* (Faber & Faber, 1967)

Gray, William, *Seasonal Occult Rituals* (Aquarian Press, 1970)

Harrison, Michael, *The Roots of Witchcraft* (Muller, 1973)

Insole, Alan V., *Immortal Britain* (Aquarian Press, 1952)

Kipling, Rudyard, *Just So Stories* (Macmillan, 1965)

Knight, Christopher, and Lomas, Robert, *Uriel's Machine* (Arrow, 2000)

Leland, Charles Godfrey, *Aradia: or The Gospel of the Witches* (Daniel, 1974)

Michell, John, *The View over Atlantis* (Abacus, 1975)

Murray, Dr Margaret, *The Witch-Cult in Western Europe* (Oxford University Press, 1971)

Regardie, Israel, *How to Make and Use Talismans* (Aquarian Press, 1972)

Rodway, Howard, *The Tarot of the Old Path* (Uranio Verlags AG, 1990)

Russell, Prof. Jeffrey B., *A History of Witchcraft: Sorcerers, Heretics and Pagans* (Thames and Hudson, 1980)

Scott, Sir Walter, *Letters on Demonology and Witchcraft* (Murray, 1830)

Sharp, William, *The Works of Fiona Macleod*, Vol. 7, Uniform Ed. (Heinemann, 1919)

Skene, W.F., *The Four Ancient Books of Wales* (Kessinger, 2004)

Valiente, Doreen, *The Rebirth of Witchcraft* (Hale, 1989)

Vinci, Leo, *Talismans, Amulets and Charms* (Regency Press, 1977)

Vogh, James, *The Thirteenth Zodiac – The Sign of Arachne* (Granada, 1979)

Woolf, Virginia, *The Diary of Virginia Woolf*, Vol. 5 (Hogarth Press, 1984)

Index